"These are not prayers for those who want to impress God with their piety. They are real prayers for real people who are ready for real communion with God. I have not encountered such honesty in prayer since David's Psalms."

—M. Craig Barnes
Professor of Pastoral Ministry,
Pittsburgh Theological Seminary

"In a day when some think questions about faith are incompatible with confidence in the love of God, Dumbfounded Praying comes as an antidote to such foolishness. Certainly, to suppress questions is to risk dishonesty and pretense, or worse, fall into the temptation of actually thinking we have achieved Omniscience. Children have no conflict between feeling loved and asking questions. It is natural to them. Harold Best's book is a model of childlike faith full of prayers free to ask anything yet always arriving at confidence in the love of God. Nevertheless, its themes are adult in their complexity and range. The author has unlocked doors some of us have longed to open but lacked the courage and honesty. These prayers embody a faith that looks to God as guide through the labyrinthine ways of the heart and they rise to worship when finding Him there. They are textured with laughter and tears, and remind us that when a prayer is uttered it becomes a holy place and as well a safe place. My faith is enriched by this book."

—Jerry Root
Associate Professor of Christian Formation and Ministry,
Wheaton College

"Like the ancient narrative of Jacob at the brook of Jabbok, these prayers invite us to wrestle with God. They invite us into the intimate personal reflections of a Christian leader known for challenging us all to deepen our walk with Jesus. This work is not only an invitation to read, but also to write—to take the time to articulate the deepest groanings of our own hearts. May the Holy Spirit bless us all as we live and pray before God's face."

—John D. Witvliet
Professor, Calvin College and Calvin Seminary

"Had Saint Peter and the Baptist collaborated on a book of prayers, they likely would have left something akin to Harold Best's *Dumbfounded Praying*. John's confessions ranged from 'I am not worthy to unlatch your sandal,' to 'I'm not so sure you're really the Messiah.' And the distance between Peter's boasts and his self-condemnations gives new meaning to 'bipolar.'

Such is the range traversed by Harold Best's prayers. They implore God to convert gnawing doubt into a child-like exhilaration of mystery and adventure. With the importunity of Isaiah, he begs God to turn anguish of the soul into passion for the Christ. He intones Peter, *kneeling* before Jesus and a huge pile of fish, wracked with unworthiness, as well as Peter *standing* before Jesus, saying, 'Lord, you know I love you.'

The eloquence of *Dumbfounded Praying* makes the book worth reading, if for no other reason. But the towering symbolism and content of these prayers will give readers impetus to work out their stuff, *all* of their stuff, in the very presence of God. I don't have the poetic capacity to pray as Dr. Best prays, but his is the prayer of my gut if not my heart.

'O dearest Friend, might Smiter-Healer, trusted Creator, Mother to my breast-hungry heart, Father to the cross-broken Christ, Author of my salvation, hear me. Hear me when no words exist because none are clean. Hear me when no groan suffices and no breath is left. Let me pray it this way: Purge me, chasten me, refine me, that I may offer, while I offer, until I offer pleasingly to You, in whatever way your inevitable goodness prompts.'

Harold Best prays like a redeemed wreck, which he is, just like all the rest of us shameful sinners who have found salvation in Christ. With little caution and much beauty, he gives voice to our hopes, fears, and questions. I trust many people will pray these prayers of longing and desperation, longing and desperation to stand in the pleasure of our triune God."

—Bill Robinson
President Emeritus, Whitworth University

Dumbfounded Praying

Dumbfounded Praying

HAROLD M. BEST

WIPF & STOCK · Eugene, Oregon

DUMBFOUNDED PRAYING

Wipf & Stock
An Imprint of Wipf and Stock Publishers
199 W. 8th Ave., Suite 3
Eugene, OR 97401
www.wipfandstock.com

ISBN 13: 978-1-60899-662-9

Manufactured in the U.S.A.

Dedication

To Reverend Robert Liljegren

 OB LILJEGREN WAS MY pastor for over a dozen years. During that
time I had the good fortune to work with him as choir director and
occasional organist.

Bob's sermons were models of truth-telling, conviction, and crafts-
manship. The gospel he preached was Christ's gospel, biblically spelled
out and unequivocal. His sermons were freighted with clarity, nicely
balanced, never overloaded. And, thank you Lord, Bob never gave the
impression of trying for "The Masterpiece." He went about his work as
a craftsman would, humbled in his calling, daily in his shop, savoring
its aroma, working away one step at a time, each carefully and patiently
roughed out and brought to the good fit that good craftsmen cherish.

Bob's pastoral prayers were near-masterpieces. They were written
out, but delivered intently and flowingly in the manner of a skilled extem-
porizer. He made reading into its own gift, but kept it subordinate to the
deeper task of talking to the Lord—topic by topic, idea by idea— on behalf
of his people. I cannot recall a Sunday in which the pastoral prayer came
across routinely or haphazardly. I soon began to anticipate it much as I did
the sermon to follow. Bob stood in stark contrast to those whose all-too-
typical Sunday prayers are clichéd, unimaginative, and routinized.

When Bob announced his retirement from the ministry, several of
us wanted to find a permanent way to honor him. We came up with the
idea of having his pastoral prayers published, even if this turned out
to be a local undertaking. We asked his wife, Mary Lou, to approach
Bob and "innocently" inquire about his prayers and the possibility of
actually getting and going over them. Bob quietly told her that he didn't
have a single one. He went on to say that after each worship service,

he destroyed the prayer, not wanting to be tempted to fall back on it in the future, and—bless his Christ-humbled heart—he didn't want any of them to become idols.

And here I am now, writing prayers for publication! What cheek! But I do so, partly at least, as a tribute to Bob's great gift and greater humility. I ask God to work a work within that releases me personally from what I have written, so that in spirit if not in fact, I can walk anonymously in the steps of Bob Liljegren and his fervent desire to pray well and to be forgotten in his praying. I admire him greatly and after all these many years of separation my love and esteem for him continue.

Prayer

Master, they say that when I seem
      To be in speech with you,
Since you make no replies, it's all a dream
      —One talker aping two.

They are half right, but not as they
      Imagine; rather, I
Seek in myself the things I meant to say,
      And lo! The wells are dry.

Then, seeing me empty, you forsake
      The Listener's role, and through
My dead lips breathe and into utterance wake
      The thoughts I never knew.

And thus you neither need reply
      Nor can; thus, while we seem
Two talking, thou art One forever, and I
      No dreamer, but thy dream.

—C. S. Lewis

Foreword

I GREW UP IN a church culture that insisted that the only *real* prayer was unscripted. Spirit-filled Christians prayed "from the heart." Spontaneity was a mark of sincerity. Improvisation was the norm. Free prayer from the congregation was encouraged. Pastors had no corner on prayer—there was as much prayer from the pews most Sundays as there was from the pulpit. But as I moved through my adolescence, I began to ask questions. How did all this spontaneity manage to result in this end-less repetition of tired clichés? Why did so many of these prayers sound the same week after week? Why did so many of these prayers consist in telling God what was going on in the world and neighborhood and then giving him advice on what to do about it?

It seemed to me pretty thin soup. But bit by bit I was introduced to ways of prayer that weren't reduced to telling God what to do and reporting the gossip of the neighborhood. *Written* prayers. The Psalms to begin with. Then the prayers of Jesus. Prayers that I didn't make up on the spot but prayers that included me in a vast community of prayer. The first extra-biblical book of prayers that I made my own was John Baillie's *Diary of Private Prayer*. There were others along the way, the most recent one this one, *Dumbfounded Praying*, the book you hold in your hand. I wish I had it sixty-five years ago when I was edging my way out of adolescence and looking for help in using a language that was reverent in the presence of a Holy God, quietly attentive to the Mystery of the Trinity.

These are prayers, *written* prayers, prayed and written by a fellow Christian who does not presume to teach me how to pray, who does not try to figure out what makes prayers "work," whatever that means. Simply prayer. Unpretentious common prayer immersed in the everyday business of being present to God. Dr. Harold Best provides his praying imagination with a pen and gives it permission to wonder and meander through the entire landscape of his life—people he meets, feelings that come and go unbidden, unnerving doubts and perplexing questions. It is unmarked country, without signposts, what Auden once named "The Land of Unlikeness." He wanders, but he is not lost. His pen is a compass. Informed by a long lifetime of meditation in Scripture and deeply nurtured in a community of worship, his writing keeps him oriented to the Way, his True North.

His pen also serves as a probe. Harold Best's pen is particularly "probing" when he goes after "sins that hide other sins." He prays, "Dear Jesus, I know they're there because Your Word says so, but I've been taught to concentrate on the sins I can draw a picture of or measure and these do a very good job of diverting me from the real truth about the real dark . . . the sins most likely to be hidden or disguised, often masking as virtues, the ones we are more apt to get by with, hard to measure and even to prosecute . . . pride, unbelief, jealousy, envy, narcissism, lust, covetousness, spiritual idolatry . . ."He is under no pious illusions as he writes these prayers: even prayer itself can be a "sin that hides other sins." And so with pen in hand, in these extended conversations with his Lord Jesus, Harold Best probes, gets under the surface and lays out for rumination and reflection and correction before God these sins that so easily and often masquerade as virtues in the company of God's people.

Prayer is as natural and simple as language itself. The only difference between prayer and our mother tongue as we commonly use it is that in prayer God is a major voice. We all learn language without formal instruction. We are wondrously created with all the bodily parts in throat and mouth and ears that are necessary to speak and listen. But we don't learn it out of a book. We learn it in the company of our parents and siblings and neighbors. And friends like Harold Best. When we go to school to formally "learn" the language, a good bit of the spontaneity leaks out.

Prayer is a natural and authentic substratum of language. But there is an irony here: prayer, language at its most honest, is also the easiest language to fake: We discover early on that we can pretend to pray, use the words of prayer, practice forms of prayer, assume postures of prayer, acquire a reputation for prayer, and never pray. The devil is not so foolish as to attempt seducing us into not praying. He simply shows us ways to pray that have little or nothing to do with God: fantasy prayer, impersonal prayer divorced from any relation with the God revealed in Jesus. Prayer that tells God what to do but never stays around long enough to listen to what he is already doing. Prayer that amounts to nothing more than being nice before God in the presence of other Christians. Our "prayers" so called become a camouflage to cover up a life of non-prayer. Some of us get by with it for a lifetime and never get found out.

The difficulty in praying is being ourselves, just ourselves, our unlovely and unspiritual selves, our doubting and cynical selves.

But maybe the most distinctive feature of this book of prayers is Dr. Best's wide-ranging, colorful, multifaceted, and energetic imagination in the practice of prayer. The sentences are sinewed. The metaphors are fresh as dew. There is not a cliché in the book. He notices everything and prays everything he notices, which is to say that he brings his life into conversation with Jesus and the entirety of scriptures. These are long prayers, but not self-centered, not self-absorbed. I promise you, you will not be bored. You will find yourself, as I do, in the company of a man who knows how to enter a conversation at a most intimately personal level and then listen. In prayer, listening is required. These prayers come out of a lifetime of listening, listening in the company of the Trinity, listening to the revelation in the Scriptures, listening to the voices of friends and family and companions. The prayers are leisurely and ruminative, gathering everything in the dailiness of world and work, family and friends and church, and mixing it into everything in Genesis and Psalms and Isaiah, Jesus and Peter and Paul. I find this nothing less than astonishing. I have never come across anything quite like it—*this* earthy and *this* reverent. I am going to be reading and praying these prayers as a neighbor and companion to Harold Best for the rest of my life.

Eugene H. Peterson
Professor Emeritus of Spiritual Theology
Regent College, Vancouver, B.C.

Acknowledgments

SOMETIMES THERE IS ONLY a slight difference between a dedication page and an acknowledgements page. "Without whose help this book would not have been possible" doesn't quite tell the truth. Books without help are possible, they're just not that good. So with the present undertaking; if it approaches some kind of goodness, it's in large part because of help from the outside—from others—as significant parts of the whole.

I mention first an elegant lady, loving, intelligent, and forbearing. Her name is Myrna and she is my wife of less than two years. We have both lost spouses, each to cancer. During our courtship, we came to understand the rightness, the godliness even, of continuing love for the ones gone from us. We continued to grieve their going, even as something refreshingly different, yet mysteriously the same, grew on us: unmitigated affection and an uncommon happiness in discovering that love is a Pentecost of languages. We quickly saw that we were not replacements for someone gone away, but creatures new to each other, fresh, different, gifted, flawed, and forgiving. And so it is, thanks be to God.

The greater part of *Dumbfounded Praying* was written within the last year, and its publication will almost coincide with our second anniversary. Even if the dates don't quite coincide, I want this book to be a gift to Myrna. She has read and re-read many of these prayers, both critically and devotionally. But more to the point, she has been my loving wife and friend all along, always concerned as to how my writing has gone, always asking, always confirming, and always at work in her own prayer life. I love her and thank God for her.

Then, to another lady I direct some words, again torn between dedication and acknowledgment. Susan Best Lauer is my daughter, mother of four, artistic—not "inclined" but gifted—a deep thinker, extraordinarily good with words, willing to wrestle through her faith, expressing herself and her sojourn candidly, hopefully and truth-<u>fully</u>. She has helped me edit this book, prayer by prayer, confirming here, questioning there, trimming, repositioning, less as a daughter than a co-conspirator, a companion and a first-rate friend. Over and over again her insights and sense of clarity have been brought to bear on some rather clumsy, sometimes snippy work. And other times, contrary to her own preferences, she has allowed me more than a touch of what, in better writing, is called poetic license.

But the daughter part—that flesh and blood part—I'm honored to say, trumps everything else.

Harold M. Best

A Welcome to the Reader

CHRISTIANS LIVE IN TWO directions at once. In words of Scripture, we live *unto* the Lord and we live *in* the world. We do so in a seamless triad of faith, hope, and love. Within this, our worship, witness, ministry, teaching, learning, work, repentance, growing, and praying take place. Just as "unto the Lord" spells out the saving direction and final significance of our lives, prayer is the cradle into and from which we pour out to God everything about ourselves, our world, our place in it, even while surrendered to God's will for it and for us.

No subject is off limits in prayer. No one is unwelcome or excused from its privileges. No language is barred. There are no aesthetic barriers, no secret code-words, or time constraints. Silence, groans, sighs, words, awkwardness, eloquence, disjointed agendas, unfinished thoughts, strange questions, ecstatic utterances, laughter, tears, importunity, doubt, contemplation, surrender, and obedience—these are what make up our side of praying, our speech with God. And sometimes our most effective praying takes place when we don't even realize that's what we're doing.

On God's side He, too, is in speech: within His Triune Person *about* us, in His revealed Word *toward* us, and in the work of His Son *for* and *in* us. His conditions are few and gracious. He wants us, invites us, works within us, and teaches us to pray. He asks for our trust even when it seems that there is nothing but doubt to speak in its place. He may even introduce doubt if our trust becomes a bit too heady and easygoing. He assures us that we need not invent new ways of praying or think up things that no one else might think of. Prayer is not a test of intelligence or creativity, but a continuing sign of hunger and wonder—and the inborn desire to talk.

Because God is Truth and because there is no condition—on our side or His—left unattended in His Word, He asks that our speech with Him have no other wellspring than what He has already said in His

Word, for within it we find ourselves, every last bit of ourselves, and everybody else. And we find Him: Father, Son, and Spirit, walking within all conditions, close by, rising above, cleansing, conquering, healing, promising, pruning, chastising, forgiving—not just once in a while, not just by chance—but unrelentingly and in unblemished integrity.

He wants us, then, to use His Word the way our Savior used it to shut Satan down in the wilderness, the way the prophets rehearsed it in their prayers, the ways the psalmists cried it out, the way the apostles lived and inscribed it. He wants us to know that as all these usages were painstakingly summed up in His Word, the Holy Spirit stamps today's date on them and keeps them alive for us. He continues to bring them to finest sheen and sharpened edge, and faithfully invites us to their rightful use at just the right times. He wants us further to know that as we pray, even if only to yearn toward Him or whisper "Abba," He hears, He knows, He works, He completes, through the twin advocacies of Son and Paraclete.

Dumbfounded Praying is not meant to be just an eye-catching title for this book. Dumbfounded is a fascinating, flexible word. In the mystery of facing the Lord, in confronting ourselves and the world, this word takes on the likes of puzzlement, wonder, incomprehension, doubt, trust, joy, anguish, peace, paradox, assurance, hunger, forgiveness, patience, power, redemption—there's more. But above all, the glory, majesty, purity, holiness, love, mercy, forgiveness, grace, patience, power, imagination, all-knowingess of Father, Son, and Spirit are dumbfounding beyond understanding, beyond measure, and beyond any earthly device we might employ to describe and laud them. For everything about God is dumbfounding; nothing about Him is routine or commonplace. It is only by His loving mercy that He hides His fullness from us, otherwise, in the words of the Roman Catholic theologian, Hans Urs von Balthasar, "Divine Love can appear in such an overwhelming way that its glorious majesty throws one to the ground."[1]

I did not write this book to show what I know about praying. To the contrary. I am a flawed and needy pray-er, still in the lower grades, beset with intellectual waywardness and spiritual aloofness, often afraid that I don't mean what I say, perplexed by the damage we do to our neighbors, vexed over the vagrant ways of the church, bound up with my

---

1. von Balthasar, Hans Urs. *Love Alone is Credible.* San Francisco: Ignatius Press, 1963, pp. 56–57.

self-enclosed history in place of God's, and ever so prone to make Him into a larger version of any number of persons, places, and things. Even as I write this introduction I feel no little amount of hesitation, wondering why I have had the gall to offer what so often falls short of the very goals and ideals I treasure.

However, taking the time—the many hours—to write and rewrite these prayers has shown me how praying can change when thinking things through before the Lord takes priority. I've discovered that otherwise shallow and paper-thin praying can change through extended thought. When I attempt to go deeper; when I begin to put scriptural and conjectural meat on the bones of the usual, things become more panoramic, more unsettled, more rigorously tested, more scripturally reasoned and accepted. Likewise, I have been taken to the very edge of faith where the evil one comes in with powerful suggestions that *the* faith is not what it is cracked up to be, that *my* faith is a shaky concoction that stands little chance before God. But I've also learned how refining and up-building these exercises are, especially as I test and re-test the promises, the patience, and gentle firmness of God, the regularity with which His Word takes over, and His Spirit confirms its unassailable wholeness.

I believe more than ever that the age-old craft of writing prayers should be re-visited by all of us, for it accomplishes three things. First, the writer is literally forced into levels of thought, scriptural usage, and architectural cogency that are not possible in the kind of spontaneous praying that one usually does in private, and sad to say, is often found in the typical pastoral prayers in corporate worship. Second, even though writing prayers takes time, time is the very thing we need and must take to bring prayer into a greater sweep and cogency. But third, what goes around comes around: the more we tackle and work through the really tough issues and the more we force these into thought-out and written form, the more skilled we can become in extemporaneous prayer.

Many of the prayers in this book were written because of my need to talk to myself in front of God as I try to work through seeming contradictions and inconsistencies, for example, why He has not intervened more in the many messes that the body of Christ seems so bent on creating, why so many practitional definitions of right and wrong (sin and no-sin) have come, gone, and shifted within the church over the centuries. I am puzzled by the outspoken disagreements that gifted theologians have about the very Word of God they all agree <u>is</u> the Word of God. Hence, more than one prayer is sworn to the varied but inevitably complementary ways Scripture asserts so very few things, outdoing theology yet showing its necessity.

Here and there, you will find instances where it appears that I am stretching Scripture, and you may wonder whether to agree or call for correction. However, I believe there is a difference between pushing to the very edge of Scripture and second-guessing it or twisting its fundamental meaning, between taking liberties *with* and finding liberty *within* the very essence of God's Word. Several prayers contain true stories that no one praying privately would ever need to remind God of. They are for you, the reader, so that you can see more directly into the prayers that issue from them. There might be a lesson here: maybe we should take more time telling God stories because, as we think them through, as we pace ourselves, circumstances slow down a bit and real time memories join with and even intensify intercessory thoughts and petitions. In the Old Testament, we find God telling and retelling the Exodus story to His wayward people, and in the Psalms, Israel's stories are repeated back to God even as He is being lauded for His enduring mercies and frightful judgments. Jesus told story after story; the Gospels are superlative books of stories, and come to think of it, telling God stories is what a child would easily do.

Now and then it might seem that I let my imagination get away with me. But what better food for the imagination than Truth itself? There is so much to talk over with God, whose imagination can never be outdone. As Christians, we are privileged, obligated even, to forge unexplored connections, to build new propositional and narrative shapes, to humbly say something like this to the Creator: *"Dear Lord, Your word is eternal; it is true. It cannot be broken. I honor it and pledge to remain faithful to it. In my writing, thinking and praying, may I offer You the workings of my mind and the creativity that You have so generously put my way? May I walk alongside David and Jeremiah and St. Paul in their quest to know You and make You known as variously as possible? I do not pretend to being inspired by Your Spirit as they were, but I can ask that His light will shine on my imagination and open it to a few more of the countless possibilities that Your Word excites."*

To whom else can we turn but to the kind God, the perfect Listener, the patient One whose mind and imagination are limitless, the God who may correct, but never scoff? To whom can we go better fit to listen, to respond, to counter-propose than the All Wise Creator? Who is there beside the Son of God in whom all the treasures of wisdom and knowledge are stored? What better way is there of talking with God this way than through private prayer, where the innermost matters can be unashamedly opened up, taken apart, and put back together?

Finally, I hope that the length of these prayers (let alone this introduction!) will not deter readers from engaging with them. I realize how short the Lord's Prayer is, and not without a flash of envy, I feast on the prayers of the great liturgies. The collects of the Anglican prayer book in particular instruct me with their eloquence, precision, pungency, and formulaic genius. I will never pretend to these heights, although I believe that all seriously praying people should practice praying this way and should learn to improvise within a strict formal and aesthetic perimeter, if for no other reason than the discipline it offers. And with faith as the substance and the Savior as the Advocate, every syllable from every time and place will be turned to richness and effectiveness before the good God to Whom they are offered.

Thus, I ask the reader to bear with me and to understand that all prayers, on our side of it, inevitably fall short, even the best of them. But that's why we have the Paraclete; that's why we have an Advocate, isn't it?

1

"Father, I thank You that You have heard Me,
and I know that You always hear Me . . . "

—JOHN 11:41B–42A

DEAR JESUS,

How did you pray, sovereign Christ? I mean when you were alone, having preached through another desert day, left friendless and fruitless after teaching your heart out to the un-choosing chosen? Did you kneel? Did you stand? Did you lie down on cooling green and fight sleep, or were you kept alert in a way that escapes me? Did your mind wander? And if it did, was it from one sweet truth to another, your whole heart, your tired heart, locked on to the laid-aside wonder of heaven's thunders? What was it like to pray to the One with whom you are one, to ask Him to see you through the very things to which the Three-in-One of you had agreed from the eternities? How did your Man-faith and your God-sight get along? Did the Accuser, the counter pray-er, try to out-pray you? Did you ever wonder if heaven was a brazen echo chamber, with no windows, no door? If you were tempted beyond all tempting for forty days, did this mean it was all over on the forty-first, or did you live thirty-three years with a giggling cackle in your ears and you prayed through—clear through—and then beyond it?

Dear praying Christ, are these questions worthwhile, or am I just telling you what it's like when *I* pray, and you never went through anything like my dumbfounded utterances? But weren't you tempted in all things just as we are? And since we live with temptation all around us, and if you are always with us in all of this, wouldn't it be possible that your perfected praying was jostled, and tumbled, and thrown about, by the very satanic muscle that you turned to jelly one Easter Sunday?

Savior, when you prayed, did your prayer list have big-ticket items and little-ticket items? Did you get less worked up about the Pharisees than you did about your mom when she lost your dad? Did your prayer that Peter wouldn't fail match up to your concern for Martha's busyness? What about your siblings? Certainly you said more to your Father about their numbness than that a prophet is honored, except when he's back home—or did you? Had your mind become so fixed on a doctrine of election that you quit praying for Judas? What about the woman caught in adultery? After all, you said very little, except "sin no more." Did she follow through? How did you pray for her? Or in all these things, did you simply turn to your Father and say, "Thy kingdom come," having such a firm grasp on the salvation of everybody, all at once, that you didn't need a prayer list? If light and dark were the same to your Father in heaven and your faith on earth, are the Holocaust and income tax evasion the same? But, more to the point: is your Father—are you—equally passionate about everything? If so, were your prayer moments a holy apex, a holy plateau of ceaseless wrestling and ceaseless peace, or did you let down a little for one thing and get fired up for another, as I do? I'm afraid of your answer.

But maybe my up-and-down praying is due as much to a mistaken idea about prayer, as it is to my awkward fallenness. So, this question: Is it a mistake to make a prayer list, only to get confused because it isn't long enough, or doesn't include everybody every day? Is this why (be kind here, dear Lord)—is this why I get a bit tired of praying everyday for my Viet Nam-broken, mind-sick friend, or the latest brown-out in church growth; or, overwhelming as it is, the callous, endless hatred of nation for nation?

Why do I feel guilty for my whatever-prayers, or for not praying for my suffering friend *every* day, or for collecting a whole bagful of beautiful-feet messengers and making one quick Babel-word out of it: "Bewiththemissionaries." Or would you say these same four words, but load them with so much cosmic passion that it would take your Father his very own eternal instant to stoop down to each one, one by one? Can you help me here? Is there a way that would keep guilt, vain repetition, and endless list-making from blind-siding my honest love (and I do mean honest) for praying? In your sworn love for being my Advocate, how can I hear you re-praying my prayers? How do you pray for praying? What about the Lord's Prayer? Is it just an outline, or an all-encompassing utterance, in which you—in your omniscience—gather up all the one-by-one requests that keep increasing in my heart? If I were to pray the Lord's Prayer with Spirit-driven intensity and pleasing faith, would that do it? Then, what would I do with all the left-over prayer time? If I could pray each word of this prayer with a heart overflowing with faith, hope, and love; my mind locked on yours, and my soul magnifying no one but the Lord; would I achieve a comprehensiveness that length and quantity cannot? Perhaps I could rest then, knowing that you translate each word into the all-encompassing desires you have—for the world and for me. If this is how I should centrally pray, then I could pepper the day, instant in prayer—one person, one circumstance after another—coming in on Spirit wings.

Dear Intercessor, am I on the right track? Can I find a peace that passes all understanding, and can I learn to pray in the very freedom of God who, in the words of old Isaiah, tells us to take no rest and give you no rest, until a world-wide Jerusalem comes to praise? Can I do this without going through a world atlas? Yes, I can, because you started with page one, when you went looking for two lost souls on a graying and distorted evening in Eden; and you will go through to the last page, because it is your will that no one should perish, and your Son's blood says Amen! to this, person by person.

So, dear all-wise Father, dear saving Christ, dear blessed Spirit, dear thrice-lauded Trinity: receive this questing, confused prayer. Run it through the mills that grind exceeding fine; purge it with fire; turn its stubble to precious ointment. Cause my imperfect praying to find its rest in your perfectly gracious sovereignty. Do this, please, not just because you are praying to the Father for me, perfecting it whisper by whisper; but because we have been thrown about together, you and I—you *by* my sin, and I *in* my sin. And, even though I deserve far worse than simply being thrown about, you comfort me by hearing me. I am like a weaned child taking rest, more and more rest; always near your breast, slowly stepping from its milk, to your hearty porridges and savory meat. All the while, Bread of Heaven, I taste and see that you are good: you, the eternal Staff of Life, the one who makes breakfast for wavering doubters and cursing fishermen.

2

Peter was grieved because He said to him the third time,
"Do you love me?" And he said to Him,
"Lord, You know that I love You."

—JOHN 21:17B

D EAR LORD JESUS,
If this word "dear" applied just to you, I would feel much more honest addressing you this way. But as it is, I call a lot of people dear. Then what? To whom shall I liken you? To other ones whom I cherish? Those who mean more to me than I can say? But then what? If they are truly cherished, and you are truly dear, who has the edge? What if I had no words at all, and you simply looked inside me; would you be able to say that it doesn't matter what words I use? Would you know that you are treasured above all treasures, or find that you are just one in a long list of desirables? Do I tell the truth when I say "dearest Jesus," or even "dear Jesus"? For that matter, when I hug a grandson, or touch the love of my life and say "dear" or "dearest," am I telling the truth, getting somewhere near the truth, even at this earthly level? With how much truthfulness do I speak at all? Where is the truth in my words? Can something be partly true and fully honest? Do I choose words as truthfully as I can, and once I choose them, would I give my life to know and live out their true meaning?

You were dear to Saint Peter, or so he said, and look what happened when a servant girl tried to connect him to you. You were dear to Saint John, but he wasn't quite sure if you were the one to come, or should he look for another? How many times have you been dear to me, and how many times have I turned around and endeared myself to other masters, without so much as blinking an eye?

But I still want to say "dear, dearest Jesus." And I will say this until I have no breath. I will, dear Jesus, because there is no end to these first words, these Abba words—no end to their lilt, no let-up to their song, no

4

end to my desire to say them someday without a speck of guile, without clutching some hidden trinket that doubles for you, without being held by yesterday's prizes and penalties. I want these words to be Cana words, changed to wine—crystal-new wine—even if it comes from the sullied waters of my life. For you not only make wine when you please, but you cleanse the water, even if it simply stays water. You are dear, not so much because you make wine, but because you cleanse. Even when others have their wine, I have this water—living water, shining clear, from you.

Dearest Jesus, let me put it another way. I am slowly learning that I own two different dictionaries. One, I use down here for checking spelling, correcting errors, and finding meaning, synonyms, parts of speech, and strange new words. I look up "dear," and see that according to this earth dictionary, I'm doing pretty well. Yes, you, dearest Jesus—along with my grandson, my wife, and many others—are dear.

The second dictionary is in my heart: here where you have chosen to live, in the twists and turns, where there are so many hiding places and clandestine turnoffs; in here, where you lovingly dwell, where your blood has finished its beginning work and made all things ever new to you, and only sometimes to me; here, where the merest spark prompts your smile, prompts you to call your Spirit-breath down: your quieting and crystal-clean breath, this energizing and patient breath, this Pentecostal breath.

And here in my heart—where "dearest" often means two different things: one prompted by love, and the other discolored by disloyalty— here where you dwell, my dearest Jesus (there I said it better), you know all; you know that I love you. May I then join your friend Peter at breakfast with you? May I please hear you say something like this to me: "Go ahead. Step out. Feed some more of my sheep"? May I hear you say this, even while you continue to help me say "dearest Jesus" more honestly?

Dearest Jesus; dearest Jesus; dearest Jesus…

And I haven't even gotten to the word "Lord" yet. I shrink from this word, too, dearest Jesus. If I say it with even the slightest sign of surrender, then I am promising to give myself to your every desire for me. I am swearing myself to follow you wherever you go—to drink the cup that you drink; to taste a bitter, sour wine, unlike Cana's dancing and twirling stuff—and, if needs be, end my days alongside your friend Peter; stretched out and carried where I might not choose to go. Then, my Lord, will I say "dearest" when I have no tongue to speak with and no one near to hear my words? Will I, like you did on that Friday, hold on to God, even in his absence? Will I, with you, still own Him fiercely and say, "My God!" as you did when you became homeless? Yes, I will, dearest Jesus; yes, I will.

And can you invent a new word, a resurrection word, that you can teach me honestly to say; can you call on the Paraclete to make up one single word that says "dearest" and "Lord" and "Jesus," all at once—a single harmonious word, a constant word, a lovely, rugged and ringing word, not to be found in any dictionary but the one in my heart?

Yes, you will, dearest Lord Jesus, Abba. Someday you will.

Amen.

3

I recite my composition concerning the King;
my tongue is the pen of a ready writer.

—PSALM 45:1B

DEAR FATHER GOD:
I know you know this already, but let me tell it back to you. When my granddaughter Tessa was learning about you and learning to put sentences together, you heard her one night singing these made-up words to herself: "I love Jesus in certain way." We heard her from the next room and wished that we could think this way—that we could pray out of our imagination, kind of making truth up and saying things to you that come fresh and sideways, from that queer angle infinity offers to children.

Dear Father God, teach us what it means to love you in a certain way. Teach us that this certain way follows your way; teach us to know that our Jesus, whom we are growing to love in a certain way, is himself the certain Way—the only Way. Help us to understand that this certain Way is Truth and Life; that this certain Jesus, this only Christ, this unique Son of God, loves us in an eternally certain way; that because of him, certainty breaks out everywhere, assurance leaps forward, and victory is the certain word, authored by the One with whom certainty is eternal, hard-won, and lovingly offered. Then, we can face uncertainty, if there is such a thing—can't we? Because, dearest Jesus, haven't you turned uncertainty into a non-word for us? Yes, you have; you certainly have. And maybe the strangest wonder of all, dear Savior, is that you still allow us pain, trouble, darkness, poverty, and disenfranchisement—the very things that are supposed to cause uncertainty. But not anymore, dear Christ, not any more. This I pray, and this I say certainly; help, please, help my uncertainty.

4

"Did you not know that I must be about My Father's business?"

—LUKE 2:49B

DEAR ABBA,

Another time, my granddaughter was on my lap; she was not yet able to read, but this didn't stop her from telling me that she wanted to read to me "out of God's Bible." She held one on her lap and, snap-turning page after page, told me how you raised Jesus "from his deadness." She told me about Daniel in the lion's den. When I asked her if she had any other favorite Bible stories, she said, "Yes, it's Raggedy Ann."

Why Raggedy Ann, dear Abba? Why not the Transfiguration, the feeding of the five thousand, justification by faith, Jonah, Noah, or limited atonement? Why not just at least one more smidgen of orthodoxy? She got Jesus being "raised from His deadness" right, so why not more?

Of course, I see. The rest will come to her. It has to, because if Tessa loves Jesus in a certain way and if she knows that Jesus was raised from His deadness, then she's hop-scotching right along with grizzled old Paul of Tarsus: "If you confess . . . if you believe . . . you are saved." Of course. Now she's ready to learn more and more, then more, still more, always more.

But I have a question. Why do we grownups test each other out to make sure that every piece of faith is within our grasp, straightaway-all-at-once and in exactly the right place, because, after all, we may be on sinking sand if we only know a few pieces and can't quite remember which piece comes next. Why must we press and press and press—making doubly sure, checking again, hyperventilating into our doctrinal brown bag: My neighbor, a mite too deliberate, isn't quite ready to be baptized, and he has real problems with premillenialism. Oh my! He might get run over by a car before I tell him more, and will he be ready to see Jesus?

O dear Jesus, patient and generous Jesus, help us to know how confident you are in the simplest grasp of truth; how welcoming you are to those whose faith is shown only in touching your garment; to those who say, "To whom shall we turn? You alone have words of life"; to those who say, "I didn't know there was such a thing as the Holy Spirit." Dear bent-low Christ, we're told that you'll never blow out a barely burning flax. But how often we smother the flame by forcing too much doctrinal oxygen on it—hovering over it, crowding it out, huffing and puffing the whole truth at it—while you keep your wonderful, refreshing distance and allow your Spirit enough space for his work, comfortable with his still, small voice; his voice still and always.

So, what about this Raggedy Ann business? Would you shut Tessa down for this? Would you punish me for not standing tall for truth in front of her? Should I have stepped in on your behalf and Straightened Her Out? Why was I anointed and not afraid? Had I become a simple old grandpa, party to a tale worthy of *Reader's Digest*, eager to brag on my little tyke so my friends could chortle their well nows?

Why have I come to treasure those few minutes? Was it because Tessa had a Raggedy Ann that she could actually cuddle with, talk with, and give a tea party, all the while telling her about Jesus being raised from his deadness? And how Raggedy Ann would have been safe with Daniel because God was there, too? I think so.

And when you were down here on earth and talked about lost coins and grape vines and shepherds and Jonah and mustard seeds, was it partly because, as a little boy doing make-believe with God's Bible on Joseph's lap, you might have sneaked in a story or two you heard from your cousin, and it was too good to keep from your two daddies—one in the shop, the other in heaven? And maybe you turned the water into wine a few years later, partly (only partly, mind) because, after Mary tucked you in bed, you and the sandman talked this over, and you just knew that this could happen; you just knew it could be done and had already done it over and over playing pretend? Out in the shop one day, did you carve a little donkey and make believe that someday, you would ride one? Did you and the village kids ever have a parade—with some palm fronds? Dear Savior, it hurts to continue this.

Where, my dear child Jesus, do childhood games and grownup work talk together? How do I become a little child again, in order to do a man's work? How did you, Son of Man, dearest Jesus-Friend, look back on your childhood while doing your man's work? When the fishes multiplied in your hand, when the bread kept squirming into little loaves, when you knew where to find a coin to pay the temple tax—did you remember playing make-believe this very way, as a little boy? Did you make-believe and believe all in one song? One dance? Did Torah and tale talk back and forth? Is this what it means to become a little child, for of such is the kingdom? If so, dearest Lord Jesus, bring on the Raggedy Anns—bring them my way again before it's too late for this aging grandpa-child; bring on the Tessas with their can't-sit-still, Bible-tells-me-so-there songs. Please.

Amen.

5

His praise shall continually be in my mouth.

—PSALM 34:1B

Dear God,

How good of you to make a name for yourself, that babies can say without knowing it. They can just make the sound through their slobber—sitting in the bouncy chair, swaddled in a blanket, or spitting out spinach. Everyone can say this name; all the little children in the world can say it—a couple of vowel sounds and a consonant: ba-a-ba-a-buh-buh-ab-ab-aba-abba. There it is. God's name, child's play, Jesus' Father, man's hope.

Abba; the only palindrome for you, dear Creator. Backwards and forwards, it's still your name. We can hook it up like a daisy chain: ABBABBABBABBA. Old people gone childish can say it. Jesus said it when he taught the disciples how to begin a prayer. He said it time after time to you. He taught us to say it.

But, child's play over, Jesus taught us that Abba—just one of your names and like all of your names—must finally be said as if there were no other word for you, as if your very nature were expressed in it.

Dear God, help us to say all of your names with stricken reverence, from Abba down through the roll call of all your names; especially the one that's so holy some of your children were afraid to pronounce it: Yahweh. Infinitely Named One, please keep us from dropping any of your names—Lord, God, Lord of Hosts, Lord of Sabaoth, Rock, Salvation, Shelter, Creator, Redeemer, Bread of Heaven, Holy Spirit, Paraclete, the Christ of God—as we would those of a president or a general or father or mother or brother even, letting them simply float on profane air with all other earth-words and names.

And once I say your name—each one, one by one, honestly and reverently—please grant me equal care as I make my way through every word of my prayers, from praise to petition. Let no word drop to the ground in carelessness, or mimicry, or vain repetition. And don't allow me to think that when I pray, "words just fail me," when, truth be told, I'm just too lazy and sloppy to open this treasure we call language; to hunt down words: rich words, splendid words, precipice words, sojourn words, surrender words, poet words, lost and found words, triumph words and battle words. Please, dear Lord, don't let me abuse the word "awesome" again; tie my tongue until I'm so shuddered and sundered by your majesty that I confess my long-term profanity, and I empty my word bag of lying windiness. Teach me to stutter first; to fight through to the glory of saying one word, then another, with you surrounding me, with you running ahead of my words and turning their watery worth into the wine of sanctified speech.

Keep me from taking your name in vain when I sing it. Protect me from thinking that a chord, or a pitch, or a rhythm adds holiness to your name. And if I come to a place in prayer where your Spirit—but only your Spirit—shows me another language, keep me from thinking that I've "arrived." Help me to understand that it's ABBA all over again, not Babel or strange fire or blah-blah, dum-dum, shaba-shaba rip-offs. I pray this ever so carefully, not wanting to grieve your Spirit, pleading with you to reduce me to groans, sighing silence, and bent over quiet, until I learn to say anything to you, anything, even one syllable, with transported tongue. I pray this, fearing and loving your names, through Jesus Christ.

6

He has also broken my teeth with gravel, and covered me with ashes . . .
This I recall to my mind, therefore I have hope.

—LAMENTATIONS 3:16, 21

GREAT PHYSICIAN:
I'm a bleached-out desert turd—not a soul around to take a picture, not even one of Job's buddies. I'm a stick going to stone—my tongue a wooly cucumber, my mouth Velcro, my breath brown, my eyes glued shut, my ears a tape loop of demon scratches on chalkboard. From heart to soul and back, I'm a true story gone rotten, a forgotten effigy, a wasted-out idol-worshiping idol. I don't know how to thirst, and you are a mirage.

Do you hear?

I can hear myself though, and if I'm just talking to myself, you—a shimmering mirage—might overhear. If I'm really talking toward you, ever elusive Splendor, am I just putting vowel sounds on a death rattle? Will I buy the farm muttering to a mirage? Still, if I'm bleached waste—no mirage here—then I *am* something. I am. If I am, then maybe you are, too. Is this a semblance of reason? Do you listen to reason? But I have no other way to make way. My soul cannot be shut down, my heart still longs and I push toward prayer.

From out there, from a nearing distance, something mumbles about dry bones, strewn about, chalky, and dissolving. The turds are long gone, but the scattered bones, the prior bones are still there. I coax and I hear something about them coming together. I stay put, knowing slowly.

What, Lord, is the difference between shimmering mirage and burning bush? The desert won't tell me, my tongue won't work yet, and my eyes are still stuck shut. But the old tape loop is fading, and I'm beginning to hear another one:. . .AT. .TIAMI . . .THA. . . TIAMTH . . . ATI . . . AM THAT I AM THAT I AM.

The next step is Jesus, this I know.

7

By this we know love, because He laid down His life for us.

—I John 3:16a

Dear Loving Father:

I love you at the expense of my life and everything surrounding it. I love you, though you slay me. I love you that I might loathe everything not-you. I love you at the expense of every good thing that I have come to love and everything you would not have me love. I love you even at the expense of everything to which I have sincerely attached your Name and, according to my understanding, undertaken to your glory. Forbid, at whatever cost, that I should someday say "Lord, Lord," and you tell me you never knew me. What I'm trying to say is that, if necessary, you burn me hollow, taking out everything that I have heretofore called love, so that you may burn into me everything you love; this time, with the fire of Christlikeness—his pentecosting fire. Grant, please, that this fire will be your double cure: purging and enabling, indistinguishably Fire within fire.

To the extent that I do not tell or understand the whole truth of this prayer, please, dear Truth—eternal enemy of all untruth, half truth, and lukewarm truth; Redeemer of knowing and unknowing hypocrisy— come to me, in whatever way seems good to you. Transform; no, create newly. I want more than a changed heart: I long for a new heart, even if it beats in complete solitude—no friends, no money, no status, no family, nothing—no-thing—but Jesus, the Spirit, the Father, Three-in-One, All-in-All; eternal company in an empty world, made to overflow with your glory.

O dearest Friend, mighty Smiter-Healer, trusted Creator, Mother to my breast-hungry heart, Father to the cross-broken Christ, Author of my salvation: hear me. Hear me, when no words exist because none are clean. Hear me, when no groan suffices and no breath is left. Let me pray it this way: Purge me, chasten me, refine me; *that* I may offer, *while*

I offer, *until* I offer pleasingly to you, in whatever way your inevitable goodness prompts. If I walk in darkness, and for as long as I might, let your glory shine on me *only* that others will be drawn to the brightness of the shining: dark on the inside, bright to those around me. When all is said and done, my life, my spirit, are entirely at your disposal—into your hands I commend it—because I know, I am knowing, and always will know that you have never abused anyone, that your chastening is the guarantor of healing, that your purity alone will drench me through Jesus—the Christ of God, the Living Water, the great Physician, smitten of God that he might heal the smitten. I trust you.

Dear God, I join that pestiferous psalm singer when I say, "It is time for you to act."

Kyrie eleison, Christe eleison, Kyrie eleison.

8

"Let the little children to come to Me, and do not forbid them . . . "

—MATTHEW 19:14A

DEAR CHILDREN'S CHILD, DEAREST Jesus,
How casually we talk about single moms, single dads, coupled singles singling each other out, married couples single soon, coupling and uncoupling; with *ciao*-chirping, *loveya* on the cell phone, and *awesome* at the ready for anything larger than zero. Meantime, child Jesus, what are our words for the little children who slip into the picture and are edited out—well, partly edited out—by the uncouplers, and touched up by weekend visits and family counselors?

So dear Christ, knowing my own propensity for walking away from this or that, from him or her, I want to intercede for the deserted, for the single moms—running their arches flat waiting tables, at the mercy of the tippers, trying to make minimum decency out of indecent minimums. How do they do it? Dishes running up their arms like shake shingles, bottomless coffee mugs, sticky Formica, "I-said-with*out*-mayo," or "Are the cooks really cooking today or just planning on it?"

And single dads: harder to find, but here and there at IHOP or Denny's, awkwardly wiping syrupy mouths and donut-glaze noses—logger's calluses, mechanic's hands, broken eyes—going about this and that; impersonators, awkward substitutes for the calm of a softer hand; husky voices trying to say "There now"; wanting her back at least as a mother, but unsure of the wife part.

And Lord Jesus, what about these trendy, ho-hum, boyfriend-girlfriend, live-in, try-it-out baby-makers? What about the children the babies become? What will they ever know about the comfort of fidelity and permanence? How will they grow up? Dear Lord, please break into their lives with a godly whisper or a firm hand that leads them to purity and constancy. Help them to understand that love is more than "working on a relationship." Sponge away the scars, straighten out the twists, and dissolve confusion. On all who own the privilege of intercessory prayer, place the full sorrowful weight of the live-in-live-it-up sins against children. Likewise, Father, please intervene as never before. Through a remarkable visit of your Spirit, bring young and old back to the gospel of purity, chastity, noble courtship, and Christ-honoring marriages.

At the same time, Lord, help us to love those who, blinded and high-handed, see it differently; those who have crafted a norm out of fornication and adultery. Lord, keep us from magnifying the separation they have created between your laws and their behavior. Help us to remember that all sin, our sin, is equal under your law; that we, as miserable offenders, can only pray for them in the humbling reality of repentance and forgiveness.

And Lord, deal strongly, mightily, but mercifully, with the big-name super-star culture shapers—self-anointed narcissists—whose charisma and life-ways are so wrong, so fascinating. If it is true that they actually lead us around by the nose, reverse their ways and convert their leadership. If necessary, Lord, take them down hard and rough them up, only because you know how to raise them again into the beauty of holiness and newness of life. I do not ask this for the sake of personal indignation, but for the children and young people whom they so quickly attract and easily influence. For, it was you, O Christ, and not us, who said if anyone causes any of the young to stumble, they should be weighted down and drowned, deep down in black water. Help us to pray, therefore, in your name, remembering those words of yours along with these from your friend John: "If we confess our sins, he is faithful and just to forgive our sin and cleanse us from all unrighteousness." And knowing that you alone can close the divide between being drowned and being baptized, we ask you to act swiftly and surely.

Amen.

9

Nothing is better for a man than he should eat and drink . . .
For who can eat, or who can have enjoyment more than I?

—ECCLESIASTES 2:24A–25

D EAR LORD,
    All too often, I've dipped into your grace as if it were my own hors d'oeuvres tray. How often I've made you into my special household image, no longer the Creator Redeemer, but my own hand-crafted confessor, my co-artisan. Forgive me for wanting oh-so-badly to be "a contemporary Christian," hip, up-to-date, right up there with all things cool and knowing; forgive me for folding you into this New World of artisanal-nouveau get-togethers: herbal this, spicy that, the crafted breads, the cross-bred flavors and snappy salads, the notey wines and Mule Stool beers, all in the right glass with the right talk about the right subjects. They all taste good, and so do you—right there with me, my Cana guy—"He partied, so can I."

After all, I've been told to enjoy all you've made, so why not combine you and all the rest into one handy spiritual picnic basket? Glory to God for varietal things! My goodness—specialty salt even! And all those slam-bang marinades! Thank you, Lord. Blessings on Trader Joe's and the *sotto voce*-tastey-sniffey liturgies in the Kingdom of Napa. Thank you for hazelnut-rosemary-lavender sorbets, for that new secret coffee roast, for the latest way to sauté grapes and garden blossoms—and YESSS!—that rare moment when the *en croute* has never been, you know, as awesome.

Thank you for saving me from all of the fundamentalist no-no's, and for blessing all the nouveau yes-yes's. O how good for the world to see that there is such a thing as upscale Christianity; how good that my Christian freedom fits so well with "letting my life speak." Thank you for my newly minted legalism whereby I can prove my freedom by what I can do, instead of what I don't do. Thank you for this awesome chance I have to interact with the earth and its fruits, all the spiritual oneness that a carmelized, chipotle cheese, tequila-laced whip-up brings to the Bible study group.

O, dearest Lord Christ, have mercy on me, giddy with this nouveau-everything, so easily Christianized. Please, dear fasting famished Jesus, stark Bread, everyday Manna; clear my senses of varietal lust. Be sure, please, that I'm set free from the material evidences and usages that make me look so hip and free. Break me down to your inherent holiness. Show me what it means to follow you into the desert. Show me that glorifying you begins with starvation and thirst. Show me what it means to be panting for the next breath, while I stumble toward the water brook. Teach me the shock of Martin Luther's words: "Let goods and kindred go, this mortal life also . . ."

Put things right. Lord, if others have sinned as I have, then show us together that you are the Potter, and we the clay. Forgive us for image-making, for sizing you down and turning you into our oh-so-relevant leader, for crafting you down to our societal size. Starve us that we might learn how to feast. Redeem our appetites; put heart before art, that we might seek the kingdom of God and his righteousness in spirit and truth—by the kind of faith for which there is no outside substance or evidence, by the kind of love of which you alone are Author and Finisher, and by the kind of hope that knows without wishing. Teach us the glory of a world-barren new birth—the Gospel's swaddling clothes around us, you nursing us with the milk and honey of heaven's manna and we delighting in the merest drop, growing up into the stature and fullness of yourself. Allow us the honor of being poor with you that we might, above all, know the riches in glory we have in Christ Jesus.

Then, Lord, then and only then, as we are being saved *from* this world, show us what it means to be saved back *into* it. Show us that none of these things were wrong in the first place, but that we were wrong *about* them. Then, dear Provider, then take us back to whatever bounties you measure out; to all the art and craft of taste and nuance. Let us return reverently to the next get-together; remind us that pomegranates and shiraz and grainy breads and quaint cheeses are yours, even as you give them away; that fruit comes from *your* fields and that cookery is an offering, both to the imaginative and the temperate. Take us to Cana, not so much to bow down before the wine, the roasts, and the puddings, as to kneel before you, who gives freely that we might taste carefully.

Show us how to be Christ-like in our thanksgiving and prophetic in our brunches and savory get-togethers. Let taste and testimony conjoin, so that those with whom we were once fellow showoffs will come to know that the first Feast is Jesus, himself: the Bread of Life and the Royal Wine of Heaven; that all earthy feasts—as imaginative and savory as they can be—are the merest symbols of your heavenly bounties. Then, Lord Jesus, then, bless us in every nuance and note, every latest thing that we once enjoyed from the lower reaches of paganism. Help us to realize that you were calling it "good" all along; that it was us, and not the foodstuffs, that needed changing.

And finally, provide us with the smiling grace and singing humility to give away far more than we ever consume; to cherish a drop of water with as much thanksgiving and hilarity as we do the latest micro-brew; and to be sure that temperance provides the mastery in whatever we do. O Christ Jesus, whose eternal hunger to redeem outruns ours to repent, whose bounty embarrasses our generosity, please work us hard; please show mercy to our feast, and show us your way of fasting within it. Show us how to give away before we receive. Then, dear Lord, without trying to be cute about it, help us to know that we can have our cake and eat it, too; with you as both guest and host, provider and participant; with a world of starving children and outcasts fed with more than our condescending gruels and left over Twinkies.

Amen.

10

*"God is Spirit, and those who worship Him
must worship in spirit and truth."*

—JOHN 4:24

DEAREST LORD,
Help me to understand that I cannot become reverent at the drop of a worship song, or the sparkle-ring of a Sanctus bell. Help me to understand that you are not suddenly, or now and then, holy. It's so easy to drop your Name in the middle of a hymn or during table grace or a stubbed toe. So often, when I most think I am Christian, this very thought dissolves the reverence with which I am commanded to address you. Help me to grieve—to be wounded for very love of you—over the verbal shrapnel of all who take your name in vain—in the street, in the pulpit, over brunch, on the job, or in a lover's arms. Teach me what a life of unceasing reverence is. Save me from putting on holy clothes for holy times; save me from occasional worship and now-and-then-witness.

Your word tells me that I am actually dressed in your righteousness; that I must praise you seven days, not one in seven. Your word commands me to worship you in the beauty of your holiness, in the slow-growth beauty for which I strive, in the beauty of my hunger for righteousness, and the Light within which I am told to walk. I am told that as I stay steady with your steadfastness, walking in this everlasting Light, the blood of your Son keeps on cleansing me from my sin. Please, dearest Savior, do not leave me to my whimsies. Rescue me from conformist church-going, worship-talking waywardness, and from the gradual cooling that finds its comfort in being lukewarm.

In Jesus' Name, please.

11

"For the Lord does not see as man sees . . . "

—I SAMUEL 16:7B

DEAR LORD JESUS,
        Does this sound right?
Some sins can be repeated, others can't. Some sins are pretty easy to see, easy to prove, easy to count and measure. We can get drunk just once, or over and over, but the sin is clear cut. We can steal once or make a living out of it. But stealing is stealing; it is measurable, and it is wrong. Adultery, murder, abuse, and many more sins are unambiguously identifiable and notoriously hurtful. They are as obvious as bricks. And our assessment of different people is usually based on what we can see and measure; because we make character judgments out of what we see and measure in each other, we do a lousy job of finding out what people are really like, deep, deep down. Forgive us.

But as bad as these topside sins can be, there are worse sins. They are the very worst, and they are strikingly few. They don't repeat themselves over time, they just persist. Every one of us commits them, and even in spite of your help, they hang on until we die. They're also the ones most likely to be hidden or disguised: sins that hide other sins, often masking as virtues, hard to measure and even to prosecute, except by God himself. Dear Jesus, my ego doesn't want to admit them, but I know they're there because your Word says so. I've been taught to concentrate on the sins I can draw a picture of or measure, and measureable sins do a very good job of diverting me from the real truth about the real dark.

The deep down darkness—this is where we find that we are sin*ful*, not just sinners. Here the spiritual sins fester; the inward, camouflaged, character sins: pride, unbelief, jealousy, envy, narcissism, lust, covetousness, spiritual idolatry—these are the proving grounds for the exceeding sinfulness of sin. These are the killing sins—synonyms for each other—and together they spell out the single monstrosity, the unique sin: self-worship. This is the way we are. But it's "the way we are" that took your Son to the cross. He died for all kinds of sins, yes. But more profoundly, he *became* sin; he became "the way we are," before he died for what we *do* because of the way we *are*.

Lord, you know better than I how we allow this kind of sinfulness not only to persist among the best of us, but how we actually turn it to our advantage. We use it to prove what powerful leaders we are: how entrepreneurial, how passionate, committed, charismatic, and unrelenting we are, even in the preaching of the Gospel. And we preach against these sins, even while invoking your blessing on those who make them look like gifts from you. No other sins can be manipulated this way. We might hear of a Christian leader, a deacon, a worship leader dismissed for adultery or drug usage or pedophilia, but not for being proud or self-centered or envious. We can't go there. Our self-worship is such that we can make it appear to be your worship, your Spirit, your testimonies at work within us. This is how we can make dark appear to be light, and in so doing, feed into the very counsels of the evil one; for what he really wants is to make bad things look good and good things look bad.

Dear Lord Jesus, please understand that I'm not excluding myself as I pray. I'm in this mess up to my eyebrows. We, the nobodies of this world, are just as infected as the somebodies, and can do unnameable damage in the smallest places: at home, at work, in a Bible study group, and even in the silence of our minds and hearts—hating and lusting and plotting; quietly, narcissistically, godlessly. And get this! We make sure we avoid the noticeable sins—the measurable ones—and in this way we build our reputations, keep our public record clean, and assure ourselves of acceptance among those who are in the same business of living noticeably.

Lord, it's not that we're never convicted of the deep sins, nor is it true that we never confess them nor try to avoid striving against them. We just fail to realize how preveniently evil they are. We even go so far as to take pride in speaking of how pride dominates us—that's how insidious these sins are. No drunkard would ever think of getting drunk to show that he gets drunk, but that's what we do with self-worship: we use it to confess our self-worship. God, I know this to be true, because it's true of me. And unless I am a unique sinner—not just the chief of sinners, but a sinner for whom there's no prototype anywhere—I can assume that all of us, to one degree or another, hide sin with sin.

That's how wretched we are, and that's why Jesus came. It would have been a lot easier for him to send our one-by-one sins packing, but he went where only infinity could go and as deep as the exceeding sinfulness of sin. He became the very sin that causes sinning, and only in this way defeated it wholly and eternally. If, as your Word says, all sin is idolatry, and the chief idolatry is self-worship—the self making itself into its own chief god—then—I can barely say this; bear with me, please—then Jesus, Very God of Very God, in becoming sin you became the antithesis of God himself. Dare I say this? The Son of God, God himself, became an idol and an idol worshiper together. Why else would he struggle so violently in Gethsemane, going against his very nature and taking to himself the opposite of what he is? Why else would he be completely shut off, so utterly forsaken by the Father? Why else would he cry out in eternal aloneness, and who else but the Christ could undertake this massive horror, this double mystery, this blackened paradox of becoming a false god—idolatry itself—all the while loving, worshiping, and possessing the one true God, his only God? What else could so tear at the Godhead and take the Savior to perdition but this?

O Jesus, how could you? How could you? But you did. Please fill these scattered words with all the force of your passion. Make them as truthful as you are. Please help us get to the root of things, even as you did. Purge us, burn us hollow; cleanse us with the Refiner's fire so that we might become true worshipers—in spirit and truth—leading the march against all evil until Jesus comes and completes within us what he completed on that very Good Friday.

12

Then the Lord answered Job out of the whirlwind, and said:
"Now prepare yourself like a man; I will question you,
and you shall answer Me."

—JOB 40:6–7

DEAR CREATOR:

When the cosmos was thought to sit on the back of a turtle, and a ship could drop off the far edge of the earth-dish; when the "universe" was pretty far out there, and only so large; when Solomon ventured the thought that the sum of the heavens could not hold you; when your earth and the generations back to Adam were turned to simple arithmetic and old, old was measured with a few thousand years; what were you thinking about the way we think of you? What did you see in our urge to think of your infinity as a jump ahead of the widest expanse imaginable?

Now that our minds have a multi-billion-light-year universe to contend with, look what we can do with you when we go back to Solomon's words and update them. The more some of us know about your creation, the bigger you get. Wow! Thank you, Lord, for updating us. And there are others who are so taken by the size of the cosmos that you become a near impossibility. They shrink you down, turning you and your truth into a mystical after-thought, a soft-bellied addendum to the conceits of scientific triumphalism.

In either case, we seem bent on yardsticking you. It's much easier this way, to measure your size against size itself. Lord, we confess that "bigger" is more appealing than "other," and maybe size and substance— especially the way we think of "immeasurable"—lies at the heart of idol-making. If so, we have to own up to our sin of making you into a magnificent, over-the-top idol. Look how you've grown lately! And maybe Israel's easy jaunt into making a golden calf was nothing other than wanting a localized miniature of a magnificent, super-sized, mountain-dwelling Idol; not yet Yahweh, not yet I Am That I Am, not yet Spirit and Truth. Instead, "It's this version, Israel—it's this nearby thing, Everyman—it's this that brought you out. We have a big version of him and a small one—one for the special worship times and one for the everyday, walkabout times."

What is there about us that squeezes you down by pumping you up, except our spiritualized idolatry? What is there about us that reduces your transcendence to a few majesty choruses and spiked-hair-open-collar-relevance sermons? Why is it that the more Hubble shows us and scientific brain power tells us, the more we worship our own concoctions of majesty? Is it because we try to see your infinite otherness by your handiwork, instead of by your person? Is it because we cherish sight more than faith?

Dear God, how long will you put up with all this? When will your Spirit say, "Enough!" and having had enough, take himself away from us? Or will his "Enough!" be the same Spirit that breathed on the reluctant slurry of Genesis and the dry bones in Ezekiel's dreary valley? Will it be the same Spirit that came down at Pentecost, turned Babel right side up, and made full mockery of every desire to craft the Lord and his Christ out of human conceit? Dear God, please command it to be this; for without you, without your Spirit, without your cosmos-commanding Son, we shrivel alongside our tape measures and telescopes, and measure you ever smaller, ever smaller, world without end. Dear God, wrest us from shrinking your Word down to the way ordinary words work. Take us up, up into the Word of your power and the power of your Word. Dear patient Creator, take us back to the dusty sojourning of Abraham's ways, on through the faithful, hope-filled sermons of the prophets, directly to Jesus. Take us into your very self, where the measureless is the only measure and infinity the only limit. Amen.

13

"I say to you, before Abraham was, I AM."

—JOHN 8:58:B

FATHER,

I finally learned something just the other day. Here I am an old man, slowly getting something straight about being a little child.

You know better than I do how Jesus keeps changing sizes to me. And lately, he seems to have gotten smaller. Yes, I know all about him in one way: that he stretches beyond the infinities; that his atonement is extraordinarily expansive; and that one day every knee will bow down and call him Lord. But his size—that is, the size into which my heart and mind make him—scares me, it's so tiny. I remember times when he loomed large and cosmic; I remember others when I could not get it through my mind that he could actually include me in his "I-will-in-no-wise-cast-out" welcome. And no matter what size he takes, I worry about the final laugh being on me, even though I truly believe I love him with all my heart, mind, and soul. I *do* love you, O Jesus, but why doesn't my faith-mind enlarge you, magnify you, the way faith led Mary's magnificat-heart? I want to be overwhelmed by you in such a way as to leave me with no other song but "Jesus, Jesus, Jesus . . ." So, I have been this way for quite some time, afraid that you will shrink me down because I can't get Jesus to be big enough.

But the other day, this thought came: "So what if your mind or your heart shrinks Christ down? That's what minds and hearts are very good at doing. Since when can anybody magnify Christ sufficiently?" And then, this thought followed hard after: "Forget the Christ of your mind, even though your mind may be Christ-centered. Forget, even, the Christ of your heart, though you have invited him there. Turn to God's Word and feast on its very own Christ and his magnificence. Let the Spirit magnify the Word—the Word of God, the Word become flesh, God the very Word. Let the Word lodge within you, and then, within this Word

27

and always within it, let the Word do its own first-hand magnifying. Let the Word out-step your mind, your heart. Reach, then, in hope and by faith. Let the Word be your imagination. Imagine through the Word. Don't give way to shaping the Word with your mind; don't let a short-lived heart-surge or mind-prize be your Christ-definer."

Lord, this is very simple, but it's doing its work. Now my mind and my heart are surrendered, totally given over to the force of the Word and its many words. And the Christ, pictured there in countless ways, is now the Christ—the Lord—of this hungry, crimped, but renewing mind. And, Lord, just because I am learning this doesn't mean I'll remember it that well. Keep with me, please.

Thank you, Lord of the Mind, Lord of the Heart, Word of God Incarnate.

14

And she brought forth her firstborn Son,
and wrapped Him in swaddling clothes and laid Him in a manger,
because there was no room for them in the inn.

—LUKE 2:7

O LORD,
When the psalmist set his mind on the immensity of the work of your hands, he went on to worry about how you could give him a second thought, and he couldn't see as far and as deep and as small as we moderns can. So, his estimate of your immensity must have been scaled down to his limited idea of distance and number. He didn't know how much sand there was on the shore because he didn't know how much shore there really is. He had no idea that the latest guess puts as many stars in the universe as there are grains of sand on this spread out planet. It would have set him spinning to know that our galaxy, one of a billion, is moving at something near a half-million miles an hour. He knew nothing about dark matter, black holes, billions of light-years, alternate universes, super strings, quarks and gluons. He had no idea that there are millions of orbiting things in a toe nail, or strange powers that hold things together or light up a city.

So, does infinity—your kind, not the physicist's—mean more to us than it used to, now that we have ten billion light-years'-worth of star dust to contend with? How would we write today's psalms? Because we know more than the psalmist, should we be better at lauding you? Should our choirs and worship teams—the best of them—trump those in Solomon's temple? Or does it still come down to the tiniest whisper of existence—a baby, a grain of wheat, or a silvered sip of water? These should be more than enough to bring the same rush of psalms and doxologies that the expanding cosmos can. Small and large are the same to you—dear Creator, the One to whom we turn.

And even though we're wonder-struck by the expanding size of a measureless expanse, we cannot forget the other side of size. There it is, way down: down where reality shrinks and shrinks even more; down where countless miniaturized galaxies swarm. There they are: the molecules, the gluons, the superstrings, the quarks, the photons, the waves and particles; there they are, down where bafflement and grand equations pass like ships in the night; there they are, down where infinity takes its own taunting turn; down where majesty is microscopic, inscrutable and squeaky-voiced, and size is nothing more than a sum of a zillion sneaky micro-parts. Now what do we say? Where is glory now? In a gluon? Of course it is, except it's way too small to compete with the kind of super-sized infinity to which we tune our guitars. "Though your sins be as a billion gluons, I'll forgive them." Not cool.

Let's get back to the galaxies, quick. My sins are big. Their size can only be outgunned by the cosmic, mega-galactic brand of infinity: the billion-light-year kind. And you're bigger than they are. Your grace outlasts the suns and the eons. We've got a new number: seventy-times-seventy cubed for starters, and it spins out, out, out where the west can't find the east. And our God, the Lord God, Lord of Sabaoth, Jahweh Himself, goes beyond and beyond. But not without things getting hurtful. The Lord of the cosmos went smallish. His Son took on flesh. He joined an alien speck in the galaxies and went to immeasurable hurt and forsakenness for its citizens. He was squashed like a bug by those who worshiped their brand of big, lauded their kind of infinity, and sketched out a god to fit. His Son couldn't, wouldn't, conform and we crucified Him.

Dear Lord God, now that we have a double-edged infinity to cope with; now that big has no more meaning than small; once we begin to realize that the grandeur of both big and small is still about size; now that we know as never before that the really big is made up of the really small; now that sacrilege has reached new heights among the pagans, who believe that cosmic size has outsized you; now as we Christians discover that in our idolatry, you've simply become a larger size than size itself—save us all.

After all, if our ten billion light-year knowledge pool has taught us nothing about the unity of the body of Christ, or the startling beauty in your holiness; if the awesomely large and the inscrutably small bring us no closer to a child's hosanna than it did in cantankerous Palestine; what more can you do than what you've already done? If we have failed you because we keep trying to squeeze you into the sciences; if even the most Christ-loving people can heighten their praise because ten billion light-years is more than a soup dish cosmos, or waters above and waters under waters, please show us something not of this world. Take us back to old, weeping Jeremiah when he said, "Stand in the ways and see, and ask for the old paths, where the good way is, and walk in it, then you will find rest for your souls."

Show us things that have nothing to do with size and everything to do with a Spotless Lamb, a Good Shepherd, a risen Savior, a welcoming Father, an empowering Spirit, the everlasting Word. Lord, your greatness, your majesty, your love, your grace are not about size, but about your person. Bring us back to that old path that leads us to who you are, without need of a cosmic measuring stick. Take us to your person. Do this in the spirit and according to Truth. Cause us to live in the heavenlies, where Christ is seated at the right hand of the Father's majesty, where faith, hope, and love do the talking. Allow nothing of this world or this cosmos, big or small, to pencil-sketch your being.

"Sir, we would see Jesus." "Lord, how excellent is Your Name." "The blood of Christ keeps on cleansing us from all sin." "He is risen!" "You are ambassadors, as if God himself were making his case through you." "In whom we live and move and have our being." "Let Us create man in Our image." "Beloved, love one another, even as Christ loved you." "For God so loved the world that He gave . . . ." "Adam, where are you . . . ?" The Lamb of God slain—not from the foundations of ten-billion-or-so light-years'-worth of stuff—but from the eternities. Dear God, press us, please, into these truly measureless verities, your personal infinities. Release us from upsizing your glory. Help us to see into the manger; into loaves, fishes and wedding wine; into Gethsemane, Friday's dark, and Sunday's glory with but one kind of sight: faith unto more faith. Amen.

15

"O My people, what have I done to you? And how have I wearied you?"

—MICAH 6:3

DEAR LORD,
If you were simply another human being going about daily
things as we all do; and if you were in any kind of need and longed for
some kind of help from someone, even a pittance; how left out you'd be,
if you got from others what you get from me.

Here you are: King of the universe, supreme Inventor, all-sufficient
Redeemer, unsearchably merciful and all-glorious. Here I am: numb of
tongue, shriveled in song, lazy-limbed. Here I am, given so much, par-
taker of your nature, washed in your Son's very blood, promised infinite
blessedness; here I am, so unlike dancing David, so removed from Paul
and Silas singing their shackled way through midnight, so expression-
less in the face of angel choirs and burning bush, so reluctant to hoist a
song.

I'm afraid, dear God; frightened in the face of my numbness;
frightened that I might not even know you, for how could I truly know
you without bursting open and openly? I'm afraid that the book-loads I
know about you are shut up in their own dust and self-appointed intelligence. I'm afraid that I'm not much more than a well-informed observer,
a theological walkabout with no holy clue as to what it means to see the
outside from within you.

Please, please, please expend yourself, dear God. Use your might—
an ounce is enough, or does it take all of you? Spare nothing, then. Take
whatever it takes from you and from me, that I might, even for a bursting nanosecond, enter the spangled courts of laudation and praise.

Yet, Lord, in the meantime, is my fear and grief a kind of praise-
beginning? Can you, in your mercy, see into the numbness and find a
spark, a smoking flax? Thank you for telling old Isaiah something about
this. Thank you for sheltering me in the promise that Jesus' breath never

quenches but ignites. Thank you for mercy in the smoke and grace in the embers. If there is any connection between a flax and a burning bush—and I think there is—then, Lord, I find rest as I wait, I take strength as I rest, and look to you, the I AM THAT I AM, to set me afire and lead me toward the dance. Amen.

16

You who make mention of the Lord, do not keep silent, and give Him no rest until He . . . makes Jerusalem a praise in the earth."

—ISAIAH 62: 6B–7

DEAR SAVING ONE,
 Who could ever go against your will? And who, when you say that something is your will, who could ever displace it? When we try, you laugh; at least that's what the second psalm says.

Alright then. What about your declared will that no one should perish and that all should come to repentance? When it appears that a good portion of humankind is bent on going to hell in a handbasket, and when we reflect on your Son's words about sheep and goats, or this field-hand being taken and the other left behind, we're confused, because your Son also tells us about the faithful shepherd saving all one hundred of his sheep—not a one lost or left.

Then, dear Lord, when the swarming love you proclaim bathes our hearts and minds, and the joyful thought races toward us that maybe no one could be lost—that somehow the enormity of your atoning love finds its way into everyone's final earthly breath—then the frowning ones, the labelers, accuse us of this thing called universalism, and there we are, caught in the net of "mistrusting God's Word."

But what about this mighty, weighty thought that it is your will— YOUR WILL—that none perish? What are we to do with your own words cradled in your Word? Ignore them? Assume them to be relative and hyperbolic? If so, then who can trust anything in your messages to us? Why do the exegetes pitch their tents on one of two sides of the issue, when your Word draws both pictures?

So, what do I do, conservative Bible-believer that I am? Do I pray on one or the other side of the debate? Do I pray "liberally" or "conservatively"? The more I think of praying this way, the sillier everything gets, because you are neither liberal nor conservative or anything in between.

You are God. Your Word is Truth. Your Son died for the sins of the whole world, and the mysteries of your Word come at me: *"Whosoever will may come. Jacob I have loved; Esau I have hated. As in Adam all die, so in Christ shall be all made alive. Flee from the wrath to come. I have taken away my love for Israel; no, I'll give it back. Father, forgive everyone who in Adam crucified me, because they don't really know what they're do-ing. For God has committed all to disobedience that he might have mercy on all."* Contradictions these? Self-enclosed theological positions these? Narrow prayer-paths these?

Please, God, no. Instead, help me to pray for the salvation of every lost soul, with your entire counsel in mind, with every bit of the mys-tery in mind, never minding the apparent contradictions, but resting in paradox and mystery and your sworn will. And as for me, as I struggle in prayer over lostness (and please help me to do this alongside the weep-ing, anguished Christ), who am I but a petitioner who can only seek your face on the basis of what you say, not what the savants say about you? I can only pray by quoting your words back to you; and as passionate, impatient and obedient as I can be, I say, "Dearest God: may I be allowed to stand in the breach as Moses did, and remind you that your very will is at stake; that this will, against which no one dare stand, commands that no one perish. Dear God, on the authority of your Word, I can do no other than beg you to do what your word says you cannot avoid doing. Nevertheless, not my will but yours be done."

Kyrie eleison. Christe eleison. Kyrie eleison.

17

*Christ also loved the church and gave Himself for her, that He might
sanctify and cleanse her with the washing of water by the word, that He
might present her to Himself a glorious church, not having spot or wrinkle
or any such thing, but that she should be holy and without blemish.*

—Ephesians 5:25b–27

*"Let us be glad and rejoice and give Him glory, for the marriage of the
Lamb has come, and His wife has made herself ready."*

—Revelation 19:7

Dear God,
It's one thing to understand how our persistent rebellion and
our steady rush of wrongdoing harmonize so well. Even your chosen
people, with precious few exceptions, have blown it from the beginning. You chose them, didn't you, not because they were the best, but
the worst—that is, you could have chosen any people: Irish, Chinese,
American, Brazilian, and they would still be the worst—because we are
all the worst. That's the way it is in a fallen world, and you just wanted to
start something unique and saving among us. You wanted to prove that
human wretchedness and stubbornness would in no way deter the Son
of God from becoming one of us: the meek One growing up among the
resistant, self-justifying ones; the spotless Son of Mary coming out of the
devious, splotched tribe of Judah.

But it's another thing to understand that once you've exhausted the
infinities and come down and spilled out your Blood to redeem us, and
once at least a portion of us have turned ourselves over to you, how
badly we've behaved in the name of the one whose name we know to
be the Only Name. It's another thing to sort out the disagreeable ways
of disagreeing sectarians and denominationalists, and to figure out why
there are so many separating convictions about how to walk the nar-

row Way. I can understand why there might be a wild variety of ways to worship you—a wild array of styles and vocabularies—for this is simply a reflection of your own genius for variety. But the difference between your work and ours is that you call everything that you've made good. Every atom proclaims your glory, as if with one voice. And your Word, this shining, eternally changeless composite, says changeless things— absolute things—so variously and comprehensively as to smile on a variety of emphases and protocols. But what do we do? Instead of rejoicing in a Pentecost of abba-talk: confessing with our mouth that Jesus is Lord and believing in our hearts that God has raised him from the dead, living out the Lord's Prayer and the two greatest commandments, walking in the light with him in the light, and tuning our life-songs to the faith-hope-love triad; instead of rejoicing in this solid-rock foundation, we hide it behind lesser and contingent things that may be good, but only in a subordinate way, and turn the City of God into gated barrios.

How can you stand being embarrassed and misrepresented this way? How can you allow your gospel and its sweet serenade to be turned into such self-congratulatory and clubby noise? How can you tolerate the impression that a disagreeing and divided church makes on the world?

You said you would build your church. Is this your idea of a building: leaning this way, tilting that, shored up with makeshift bracings, doctrinal tar paper, bricks, cobblestone, rust and scum, Gothic grandeur, store-front pride and black box relevance, doors open too wide, others slammed shut, windows painted over from the inside, no light in and none out?

But maybe, Lord, I speak like Peter to Jesus: "You can't let this happen to you." Maybe, I have some kind of jewel box church in mind and want everything tidy for you, when I should realize that your holiness is so unassailable, your confidence so high, and your sworn purpose so far seeing, that your only response can be, *"Child, I only deal in messes and filth. I have outlasted dirt from the eternities. I can put up with a scoffing world and a splintered church. My desire is to visit dirt as dirty as it chooses to be—even this redeemed churchy dirt, still incapable of cleaning itself. I'm going to stay with dirt until there is none around, until I choose to make it into a laundered, purged thing; shining, eternal, and clean. I'm good at this, just watch me; keep your eyes away from idols and fix them on my Son, the one made dirt who knew no dirt. Watch him: bearing it all, rising splendid and meek, eternally spotless, sure that the gates of hell will go wobbly under his lightning fist. Meantime, child, keep yourself clean; don't mistake dirt for clean, and watch out for motes and beams—you just might have them reversed. Stay on your intercessory and repentant knees until you can't straighten them. And like old Isaiah, take no rest and give me no rest until this travailing, dirty mess is turned to praise. My Word and my purpose are safe. Trust me."*

As old Sebastian Bach used to write at the head of many of his compositions: "*Jesu juva*: Jesu help." Even so, Lord Jesus, do what seems good to you. Come, Refining Fire.

18

With the pure You will show Yourself pure; and with the devious
You will show Yourself shrewd. The word of the Lord is proven . . .

—PSALM 18:26,30B

Dear True One,
 Do we have this myth-legend-fable-truth thing all backwards?
Are the word-for-word literalists, the Worded-word conservatives, the
Word-among-words liberals, the kerygma kings and redaction buffs, all
whistling too narrow a tune? If not, why do they camp out against each
other and throw dares, darts, and brickbats back and forth across the
Way? What is higher criticism, maybe, except lowered expectations; and
what is word-for word literalism except boxed-in infinity? And why do
little children—these precocious and self-centered abba-sayers—hook
facts, fancies, and impossibilities all together, anchoring themselves in
abiding trust during their mile-a-minute days and tuckered-out nights?

 Is it because we don't really trust your ways? Have we so reduced
your magnificence, your startling infinity, and the measureless distance
between your wisdom and the language-force of your words, that we
cannot tolerate the thought that myth, legend, fable, reality, history, meta-history, imagination and rock solid empiricism all fall short; that each
might be necessary and that Your-Word-is-Truth is greater than the sum
of them all? Why is it that so many differing proponents love Jesus, talk
about faith alone, loathe sin, and long for the Spirit's company? Have
you, with your enormous embrace, found a way to smile on all of them
because they are so attached to the only Name under heaven whereby
they might be saved? And why is that even the most far out critics—
the emenders, the redactionists, the splicers—keep hanging on to the
Scriptures with such persistent passion, studying and studying all the
more, worshiping and exclaiming? Why, amidst all the work and rework,
opinion and counter-opinion, are they so fascinated, so drawn? Why
don't they just turn away to another source, a more resourceful source?

39

Why is it that the motley lot of us cling to the Bible, seek your Son, and laud your majesty? Why? For certain, it's because you will not let us go, no matter what we make of you. Your Word will not let us go, whatever we make of it. Your Word stands, completely your Word, no matter how we parse, dissect, and edit. O how your Word persists! O how it draws!

So, risking a thousand frowns and sputtering interruptions, yet sworn to your Word as Truth, I wonder if we need to fret so much over the idea that myth, legend, reality, history, meta-history, but most especially your Word birthing words—please help here—are all reaching outward, straining through the distance, lighting the nearby, peering through darkened glass, everything enlivened by the One who outruns every expression, unthreatened, ready to bless, to awaken, to revive?

Why, Lord, don't we leave well enough alone? Why don't we allow all these efforts—these strivings, these marks of finitude, these over- and under-statements, these debates—to go your way; entrusting them to you, interceding all the while? And like our brother Karl Barth, why don't we close ranks, strike camp, march on and then on some more, singing "Jesus Loves Me," looking upward to Christ, as he looks down from Pentecost and across the ages, the divisions, the sniveling judgments, and honest strivings?[1]

Maybe then correction, teaching in righteousness, and thorough furnishing of all of us unto good works would flow through the body of Christ—golden bright, refined, purged, and glorifying— and you yourself would be high and lifted up, enthroned on the fullness of praise.

Amen.

1. When the great theologian Karl Barth was asked how he would sum up the Gospel and the entire corpus of his writings, he slowly began to sing, "Jesus loves me, this I know, for the Bible tells me so."

19

"See, I have called by name Bezalel . . . and I have filled him with the
Spirit of God, in wisdom, in knowledge, and in all manner of workman-
ship . . . and I have put wisdom in all the hearts of the gifted artisans."

—Exodus 31:2A,3,6B

L ORD,
I've written about this problem, I've gone over it with students
countless times, I've tried to be as biblical about it as possible, I've prayed
earnestly about my spiritual condition within this problem, and I'm still
floundering in a mix of attitude and idea. I've learned that writing about
something—solving certain problems from a biblical perspective, sharing them with a readership and assuming that my readers are better at
following principles than I am—cannot by itself clean me up. Talk and
walk don't coincide for me, even though I assume they will for others.
Either I'm wrong about what I've thought and taught, or dangerously
close to arrogant sinning, from which I seem unable to free myself. And
it could be that there are others who will pray along with me about this
problem.

It's many-sided and it's about what we call the arts. One side is art
itself, another, quality. A third is the Christian faith, and linked directly
to it, a fourth, Christian worship.

I know full well that you have high standards in everything you do.
I know that you expect us to strive hard to do things well. I'm guessing
that your Son was very particular in his carpentering and bricklaying.
He certainly was in his teaching. I've read and reread the instructions
you gave for the tabernacle's design and accoutrements; I've read about
the two temples and their grandeur. I remember your insistence in the
Old Testament that all offerings be unflawed and healthy; you were even
far-seeing enough to allow for a range of choices—down to a dove—
for poor people who couldn't afford something more expensive. All the
same, it had to be unflawed and healthy. And I also know that you would

spew anything out of your mouth, in spite of its quality, that was not offered out contrition and humility.

Yes, and to compound things, humankind from north south, east, and west, throughout all civilizations, and in splendid ways, has made what we now call art—amazingly profound, confoundedly simple, and perplexingly complex. And right up there with all this wonderful stuff is the intellectual discussion about quality. Hence, art—or whatever we want to call it—is not just art, given over to just any qualitative whim. There are these persistent things called value and taste, along with a drawer-full of labels to articulate them: great art, good art, and average art; transcendence, excellence, lastingness, mediocrity, bathos, kitsch, trash, corn, junk.

Somehow, dear Lord, through the powerful cocktail of nature and nurture, I have come to love great art and good art. And average art? Yes, I love this too, in spite of rigorous theological, aesthetic, and practitional training to the contrary. And risking a scolding from you, I have concluded that mediocre art and its qualitative siblings, while not my cup of tea—see how flip I can be?—may please you to no end, as long as earnest and faith-driven worshipers are choosing and offering it to the best of their heart-searched ability. If this is true—if you love quality, but nonetheless empty yourself of this love, for love of those who love you with the quality *they* know and love—why am I so upset and censorious in the midst of bathos and tripe? Why do I want to shut it down? Why do I want to assume that quality and spirituality are equal to each other? And why, dear Lord, are many worshipers, the so-called contemporary worshipers, picky about the wine they drink, savvy about cinema, and full of nuanced talk about the latest eating pleasure, yet careless and permissive about what goes on in worship?

Am I alone here? I know of others who get just as upset over poorly constructed lyrics, trite tunes, dumpy prayers and Cool Whip sermons. They, too, have written and taught, and when we get together on a panel we commiserate. But my aloneness is less about aesthetics than my inability to refrain from disdain when I'm in your house with my brothers and sisters, sworn to worship in Spirit and in Truth; when I'm faced with a watery porridge served up by the poorly trained, whose desire for repetition and dreamy-eyed hand signals remind me of mantra-making. See? I have an attitude, but somewhere under it I crave integrity and long to be meek and loving.

There, I've unloaded and have little clue as to where my attitude and your thinking meet. The one thing I am sure of is that, around the clock, I can be a spiteful, resentful person who loves you immensely and knows how well you know me. I can also be a jealous man, having no clue as to where jealousy for your Name and my born-again-yet-fallen jealousy stop and start. I'm confused and hungry all at the same time.

So I beg of you, please cleanse my heart and subjugate my art. At the same time, if there is wisdom and truthful principle in my concerns, give them a sweetened heart and a humbled love for everything done in your Name, whatever its quality and whatever I might think of it.

This comes to mind: "If ever I need you, my Jesus 'tis now." Please. Please.

20

For He is like a refiner's fire and like launderer's soap. He will sit as a refiner and a purifier of silver; He will purify the sons of Levi . . . that they may offer to the Lord an offering in righteousness.

—Malachi 3:2c–3

D EAR LORD,
I just talked to you about art, attitude, and the like. I want to go over the same thing another way: What if there were no word "art" and no people called "artists"? What if we just used words like painting, carving, piano playing, singing, dancing and writing, right along with plumbing, gardening, accounting, and lawyering? What if we identified people simply by what they do instead of using a word like artist or, up a peg, *artiste*, to give them that certain elevated place in culture? What if there were no special words for any kind of human work and we simply called everything work?

Then, what if worship, service, and work were three words for the same thing? Well, they are—this is what the Bible teaches—so why do we act as if it weren't the case? What if all Christian plumbers, lawyers, teachers, painters, and piano players used the words "worship" and "service" and "work" interchangeably for everything they did, and everywhere they did it? What if going to church were simply called by what it literally is—going to church? And what if everything done in church were simply called by its right name: reading scripture, praying, preaching, singing, confessing, taking bread and wine, and visiting? What if we understood that continuing worship had no special connection to any one of these things, any more than it does to any other thing—say, nursing or deep sea diving? If we understood worship this way, then as your Spirit comes on any one of us at any point in any of these actions—either in church or out of church—the alleluias, raised hands, amen-glory shouts, and supercharged quiet would spring free, unconstrained by what some habitually call "worship time" or "the worship" (meaning

44

simply the music). With every action on a level playing field, we would know that there is only one, grand, worship time. It begins when we come to Jesus, continues for as long as we live, and is perfected when we make our way into the eternities.

But, Lord, we get all mixed up. We agree that everything done in God's name and for his glory can properly be called worship, but then we go to church only to find that, no, this truth has been pinched down to just one thing: "worship time" with its "worship songs." It doesn't seem to occur to us to say "worship sermons," "worship prayers," "worship Scripture," "worship baptism," or "worship Communion."

But, Lord, that's what's implied, that's how poorly we think, and it can only end up one way: the truth of continuing worship is sold short by the bald-faced presumption of one of the parts. And compared to weight of praying, preaching, reading Scripture, baptism, and sitting at the Lord's Table, the music-as-worship part is of minor importance. It simply has no right to shape the whole. No wonder we have so many shifts and changes and debates—so much fuss over such secondary, idolized things. It might be better to lay off this musical merry-go-round: shut down the organs, turn off the keyboards, silence the omnipresent rhythm sections, close the hymn books, and put all worship teams, choirs, soloists, projections screens, and the ever-present tangle of cords, microphones, and mixers on an extended vacation. Then the commandment to "sing to the Lord" could be obeyed at home, at work, in the shower—all places of worship—at least until we get this mess straightened out.

Dear Lord, does this help? Does it at least partly explain some of the frustrations with church going? If it does, I pray that you will take charge, and impart wisdom and grace to everyone who loves your name and your dwelling place. And if there is some justification in the content of this prayer, I pray further that, instead of being arrogant or cynical, I will be a continuingly penitent believer, an incessant intercessor, and a humbled teacher seeking quiet and compassion at the foot of the Cross. I pray that I will not be found guilty of inventing my own worship compartments that, in their own way, insult the very truth I use to question others.

Amen.

21

Let us lay aside every weight, and the sin which so easily ensnares us,
and let us run with endurance the race that is set before us . . . and make
straight paths for your feet.

—HEBREWS 12:1B,13A

L ORD GOD,
Ever present and faithful Lord of each moment, overseer of
eternity, grant that this day and my sojourn within it will be winsome,
fruit-bearing, and servant-like. Allow me the high privilege of showing meekness and humility. Take me wherever you wish; place me in
company with those who don't yet know you. Let my words and actions
be pleasing to you, and, in the words of Samuel, let none of them drop
to the ground. If you decide that I am to be alone, cause me to seek the
company of those who don't yet know you, through intercessory thought
and prayer. Cause me to be deeply sobered and heavily burdened, knowing that you long for their repentance more than I ever could. I cannot
bear to forget that when your Son came to earth, seeking their company
and finding it, he showed neither loathing nor discomfort, and spared
no effort to speak of your love and grace.

Likewise, just as he was often cast into abject loneliness—unrec-
ognized by siblings, rejected by the scrupulous, misunderstood, cursed
at and betrayed by his own disciples—help me to recognize that while
I may occasionally be lonely, I will never be forsaken as he was—dying
for us all—and I will always know his company to be perpetual and curi-
ously comforting, just as he promised.

Remake my eyes, O God. Turn them toward eyes of faith. Yes, I still
want to read a newspaper and gaze at what Hubble reveals to us from
the eons; I never want to lose sight of a lilac or grow accustomed to the
beauty of my beloved. I love the look of things so much that, yes, I even
want my earthly eyes to keep seeing, just for a split second, beyond my
final heart beat.

But faith-eyes! O all-seeing unseen God; O Spirit and Truth, whose holiness is sheer beauty; here's where blindness threatens me far too soon. Here's where I need eyes—the kind of eyes that see into the unseen, that discover substance and evidence where my earth-eyes say none should exist. Save me from just talking about the heavens showing your glory instead of searching out the glory itself, the glory as of the only Begotten of the Father, the glory that grace and truth alone show forth.

O Father, increase my faith. I want to *see* you this way. I want to *serve* you this way. I want to live this way. I want to ready myself for your coming this way. As my redemption draws nigh, forbid that I look for seeable signs and measurable omens when I can steady my gaze on the One who is to come.

Even so, come quickly, Lord Jesus. Even so, Lord Jesus, open my eyes so that, looking around, I see Jesus only.

Amen.

22

"I will heal their backsliding, I will love them freely."

—HOSEA 14:4A

*The Lord is good . . . to the soul who seeks Him.
Though He causes grief, yet He will show compassion . . .*

—LAMENTATIONS 3:25A,32A

O JESUS,
    Keep me from the conceits that buddy up to my prayers for humility and meekness. Knowing me as well as you do, and teaching me more and more about myself through your Word and your Spirit, make sure that my longing for the good things runs prayer-lengths ahead of the sin that crouches at the door. Bring to mind the peaceable truth that the accuser, cackle and stab as he might, is more than wiped out by my Advocate. Scissor out the white space between the last part of Romans seven and the first verses of Romans eight. Bring them together—no punctuation marks, no stopping for breath, no pulpit-conscious phrasing—just a breathless rush of grace beyond sin.

    Then Lord, invade every prayer I utter. Help me to understand, as one old-time evangelist said, that even my tears of repentance—Spirit-drenched tears, should they flow—need to be washed in the Blood of the Lamb. Help me to understand the grisly reality of being lost and undone, only to walk smack into being found and redone all at once: evil hunting me down, but righteousness, outrunning it and sheltering me in Everlasting Arms.

    Thank you for causing these simple words to occur long ago to one of your ministers, only to find their way into a certain prayer book: "Hear what comfortable words our Savior Christ saith to all who truly turn to Him . . . ." Comfortable. *Comfortable.* Comforting, calming, comfortable words. I want to say them over and over: comfortable words; comfortable words. And then, these words follow hard after by the Comforter, the One alongside, the Savior, the One whose comfort gives voice to words that could never cast us out: "Come unto Me, all who are weary and overloaded." Comfortable words: "I will give you rest." Comfortable, comforting words: "As a father pities his children . . ." "How often would I gather you, as a hen calls her brood under wing . . . ."

When, O when, long-lasting Father; when will I sink full down into the home-welcoming truth of comfortable words? Comfort me, please, even as I try to sink down, even as I draw back, afraid that the sniggling one will once again say, "Too good to be true, sucker. How could anyone take you to her breast?" But, here I am, Mighty Lord—coming back, coming back, coming back. There you are, waiting Father—waiting, waiting, lips at work with comfortable words, arms outstretched beyond my sin.

"Sing them over again to me: 'Wonderful words of life.'"

Amen.

23

You have not yet resisted to bloodshed, striving against sin.

—Hebrews 12:4

PATIENT ONE,

Keep me, please, from overestimating how hard it is to be a Christian, because an occasional jibe or titter about you, or my love for you, comes my way. Forgive me; forgive us for overusing words like "persecution," "making a sacrifice," "being a martyr," and "going through hell." Save us from so blithely putting ourselves in the company of the truly besieged, the cross-bearing champions of history.

Likewise, deliver me from overestimating how wonderful it is to be a Christian because the S&P is up, the humidity is down, the latest study Bible speaks to my personal groove, and the worship band said it all last Sunday.

Lord Jesus, help me to tone it all down. And yes, while I may truly be besieged and put off from time to time, while at other times I can come into some really good feelings; even as brightness washes the day, help me to see further, to see even as I am seen; help me to love even as I am loved. Anoint me with the oil of humility; wash me in the waters of meekness, and though you have spread a table before me, enemies or no, cause me to hunger and thirst after the very righteousness that comes the way it came to Abraham. I pray that I, too, will believe as did he; that I will be led forward as was he, not even knowing where I'm going.

With my faith readied by your Spirit, help me to see into the bitter dark of the psalmist, the crushing weight of Gethsemane, the dim of the first empty-tomb Sunday, the torture racks, the lions' mouths, the stonings. Help me to see into these, knowing that, so far, I have been spared; knowing that I must not make room for glib comparisons between the ease of my times and the bitter sufferings of your treasured martyrs.

Then, Lord, with my faith alight, kindled by the faith of the One who loved me and gave himself for me, further ready my eyes; cause me to see the glory side, the fierce glow of empty-tomb Sunday, the peace that passes understanding, the illimitable love that takes me in on every side, the joy of the Lord becoming my strength.

And Lord, help me to understand—faith alone is true understanding—that light and dark, feast and famine, often arrive together and are the same to you. Help me to grasp the meaning of these words about my Christ: "Who, for the joy set before him, endured the cross." Allow me, shackled alongside Paul and Silas, with no release in sight, to make music in my midnights—no help from a choir, a worship band, or a window rattling organ peal—just ready-tongued and lung-rich psalm singing, with my chains as the only rhythm section.

Help me see into all of these without regard to how I feel, how my day is going, and how tomorrow may or may not be different. Let faith alone be the substance, the evidence. Cause hope to be unashamed and unconditioned.

In short, Lord of time and circumstance, let your reality replace mine.

Amen.

24

"I am the Alpha and Omega, the Beginning and the End."

—REVELATION 1:8A

DEAR LORD,
 This is what we are taught and what we believe: When we pray, you hear the prayer from all eternity—eternity at once, and at once throughout all eternity. Before I was born, you heard me praying at age seventy-nine. Before that freedom day, when I asked you to bring me to you whatever the cost, you knew I would do this from my mother's womb. I can be assured, then, that all my prayers throughout all my life are heard separately, together, now, then, and always.

Well. If you hear a single prayer forever, why can't I assume that a couple of hours *after* I take a final exam, I can ask you to help me do well in it? What about this? Can I ask you at this moment to save an irascible great-great uncle who, long before I was born, lived a scandalous life, and as far as the family knows, never came to repentance? Why can't I ask you that somehow in his last unknowable few moments he would have seen the light and, by faith, turned from darkness to its undoing? How about the unrepentant thief on the cross? Can I pray that upon hearing his cohort confess his wrong to the Savior, upon hearing the promise that they would arrive in Paradise together—can I pray that this other thief will, soon after, have come to Christ as well? Surely I can pray now, knowing that you heard me before either I or the thief was born.

Dear Lord, I'm serious about this. I understand that I could be accused of praying for the dead, or wiggling my way into universalism, or some such push-over nostrum. But this is not what I'm doing. I'm trying to test the biblical and theological doctrines of the eternity mystery in another way. I don't want to short-change the force of intercessory prayer as it answers to the rich meaning of "a thousand years is as a day and a day as a thousand years." I no longer want to limit prayer to the present or the future. For that matter, a prayer for the present becomes a prayer in the past before the prayer ends. And what is praying for something in the future, when to you it is a thing past? Why can't the ages, the eternities, be the territory within which praying should take place?

I don't want to be wrong about this, whichever way your answer might go. Instead, I'm leaning on your eternality and your magnificent watch over the sweep of things. I want to pray this way because you neither wear a wrist watch nor keep a desk calendar. I want to pray this way because, like you, I want everyone to come to repentance and no one to perish.

So, I would not only ask you to bring that irascible uncle to you, but plead with you to have brought Saddam Hussein to Jesus in that eternal instant before his neck snapped; I want Judas, sometime before he hit the ground to have seen the Light in a way he failed when he, like his eleven brothers, was stymied, cantankerous, scheming, denying, and forsaking. Lord, there are countless others for whom I pray this same prayer.

Lord, hear my prayer and if it offends you, strike it down and cleanse me.

Amen.

25

'What is His name?'

—Exodus 3:13c

DEAR LORD,
One day past, I attended a student body prayer meeting in my early years of college teaching. I was doing my best to join with each individual prayer—to keep my attention up and my spiritual eyes awake—when a new student, fresh off the street, newly come to Jesus, began to pray. From the start, his words and ideas were off the beaten prayer-path. He kept calling you "Sir."

To this day, some forty-five years later, I set my mind on that rare and haunting moment, and beg of you to teach me to think of you and to address you with new-found urges, with Spirit-breathed courtesy, and newly spun words. Help me to learn that the distance between Alpha and Omega dares me to go where formulae fail. Help me to learn what it means to talk to you without any models or protocols in front of me. Keep me, Sir, from fear of stuttering, stumbling, and skipping around from one fragment to another. Give me intercessory courage, and help me to understand that the final architecture is up to you.

Amen.

26

"And how is it that we hear,
each in our own language in which we were born?"

—ACTS 2:8

D EAR LORD,
        There's a line in the great hymn, "O Sacred Head, Now
Wounded" that goes this way: "What language shall I borrow, to thank
Thee, dearest Friend?"

My preacher-dad once told me about a prayer meeting that took
place in a small church in the impoverished mining town of Lewistown,
Pennsylvania. It was during the Great Depression, when the already
poor and hungry were taken down even further. Many prayer meetings,
including this one, were given over to asking the Lord for food. At about
this same time, the town drunk had come to Jesus, and was gloriously
converted and wondrously delivered from his addiction. He started
coming to church, but this wasn't enough. He came to Wednesday night
Bible study and prayer meeting, and all too soon, joined the more expe-
rienced believers in hearty, outspoken, public prayer.

So on this particular night, when the prayer requests turned to fill-
ing pantries, he took over; and in a loud, whiskey-trained voice placed
a huge grocery list before you, somewhat as follows: "Lord, send us a
barrel of potatoes; Lord, send us a barrel of pork; Lord, send us a barrel
of carrots; send us a barrel of flour, a barrel of lettuce, a barrel of milk."
And on he went, finally arriving at the condiments: "Lord, send us a
barrel of salt. And send us a barrel of pepper. Oh hell no, Lord; that's way
too much pepper. Amen."

Borrow language he certainly did, this dear, frank, new-cloth saint.
O Father, I can just imagine Gabriel poking Michael, and a thousand
thousand heavenly host emptying out a black hole with laughter.

I'm right, aren't I? I'd like to believe that instead of making a bad
mark in what both of my grandmas called your black book; instead of

biding your time and waiting for a chance to "by-the-way" him over coffee, you understood what we proper ones don't. You heard directly into his converted heart. Did he do this again? You know. What did his brothers and sisters in Christ think? I'm afraid I know, Lord. Have mercy on them, not him. Was there other borrowed language that he, in his new-found joy, could not repress? Could be.

But, O dearest Paraclete, honored Groaning One, who borrows no language and needs no words to articulate the urgings of our hearts, I would have loved to have heard what you said when you came to the pepper part, and how you made sure that barrels of this, that, and the other thing were pressed down and running over, as the good God poured his beneficence forth. But above all, I can only imagine how you filled this dear man's prayer barrel again and again; filled it to overflowing. And whether or not he was ever fully delivered from a certain kind of borrowed language, I'm quite sure that he made sure you were listening, whatever language he borrowed or originated. And I'm further sure that, in your goodness and generosity, you gifted him with such a flood of pure-gospel words that if he ever mentioned hell again, he would be weeping, begging you save his drunken buddies from it. This is how you work. You cleanse everything, even the old, borrowed things that are put to new use.

O Lord, unleash our tongues, and if we borrow amiss, be patient with us, then fill us with your words and your ways of saying things. Have mercy on our vain repetitions, our thoughtless clichés, our gushy effulgence, our blue-nosed correctness, our sound-system voices, and yes, the husks of unwashed speech. Replace these, by your grace, with a fullness of Truth and a flood of thoughts and words that search into the very nature of the Kingdom of God and the reign of Christ. And please, dear Lord, let none of them drop to the ground.

27

*"The LORD, the LORD GOD, merciful and gracious . . . keeping mercy
for thousands, forgiving iniquity and transgressions and sin . . ."*

—EXODUS 34:6B–7A

There is no fear in love.

—I JOHN 4:18A

DEAR FATHER OF ALL hope,

All too often, the purest saints express fear that their assurance of salvation wavers and even sometimes shuts down. These are people, dear Lord, who know and honor your word, live by faith, walk in the steps of the Savior whom they adore, love their neighbors, and tell anyone within ear shot about your grace. My mom, Lucille Best, one of the dearest Christ-centered persons anybody could know, was visited by the sooty vapors of doubt to her dying day. These people, dear Lord, knew what altar calls were; they spoke of the mourners' bench; they knew what it was to "come forward." They sang psalms, hymns, and gospel songs; they gave and heard public testimony; they grieved and petitioned in prayer for a lost world. And they had no trouble telling other people about the illimitable love of God, and his Son, who would never, never, turn anyone away. But when it came time for them to look within; when the thought of their sins broke over them—one rogue wave after another, recalling hymnbook words like "Pass me not, O gentle Savior" and "I wonder have I done my best for Jesus?" and "Don't turn Him away"—they turned inward and wondered. And shame of shames, as they compared one contrary theology to another, they were afraid; on the one hand, that they might have lost their salvation and sinned away the day of grace, or on the other hand, that they were not one of God's elect. Caught between pre-packaged theologies, many of them lived miserably, all the while loving the very Jesus whom they were tempted to doubt.

Is this Good News?

Dear Lord, some of us were brought up this way, and to make matters worse, some of us slipped and slid; we went to the altar and then we slipped and slid; we repented deep in the night and then we slipped and slid—over and over, and then again, over and over. And now, more personally: finally, when I begged of you to break in, whatever it cost—you did, and it cost. I fell in love with you and your Word in indescribably sweet ways. But then, I began to do the math. Is seventy times seven really four hundred ninety, and when did I exhaust the quota? How could God ever take back, again and then again, this spiritual chameleon—orthodox to the gills, but shifty and wayward nonetheless? God, you know that this happened to me nearly fifty years ago, and—like my dear mom, whom I enjoyed reassuring until her dying day—I, too, am visited now and then with the gray of coming to the end and being turned away.

But hear this, dearest Lord: I run to your Word in its cover-to-cover sweep. And, in spite of the accuser splattering me with Hebrews 10:26, pushing me nose first into Esau's futile seeking of repentance, and smothering me with Paul's strong-lipped thoughts about you loving Jacob and hating Esau, I have begun to read *all* your words. I read and still read Deuteronomy, and rest; I read Hosea, and I end up smiling. I read Jeremiah, and laughter breaks through lamentation. I read Psalms, and find myself both in the midst of the hurt of evil, the plea for mercy, and the anointing of everlasting forgiveness. I read about Jesus and his promise never to turn anyone away, and am amazed at how un-methodological and how un-systematically theological (or un-theologically systematic) he was.

Given my background of word-for-word sinner's prayers, I'm puzzled when I read of Jesus healing someone and saying things like, "Your faith has made you whole," or simply, "Go and sin no more," without asking for, or receiving, a hint of confession or repentance. I read St. Paul's wide welcome: "If you confess Jesus Christ as Lord and believe in your heart that God has raised him from the dead, you will be saved." I read in Hebrews that this rascal Samson is included in the roll call of the faithful. And I read and I read and I am comforted—slowly, comprehensively, and finally. That is until I turn back to multi-version Christianity and find myself confused by the number of caveats that encumber the simple words, "faith in Christ." I stumble over the memory of number-less sins, many of which were not sins in themselves—here's where the math comes in—and then, reflecting in a deeper way, I realize I almost never thought to repent of the chief sins: self-centeredness, pride, unbe-lief, jealousy, envy, deep seated idolatry.

Lord, save us from taking the simple, foundational things: "saving faith," "faith in Jesus," "justification by faith," and "walking in the light," and knotting them up with biased theologies that play games with our tenderness, strangling our hopes with hoops that your Word never in-tended or articulated. And then, when someone passes into your pres-ence, keep us from asking this question first: "I wonder if he or she was saved?" Instead, visit us with this promise: "The blood of Jesus Christ cleanses from all sin." Deliver us from weighing down the words "our faith" with undue emphasis on "our." Save us from looking inward to see how strong *our* faith is and command us into these ever-strong words: in *Christ*.

Mindful Savior, hear these words—these comforting words—"In *Christ* my faith is." O how different and differentiating. Amen.

28

Do not be rash with your mouth, and let not your heart utter anything hastily before God. For God is in heaven, and you on earth; therefore let your words be few.

—ECCLESIASTES 5:2

D EAR LORD,
If what I'm about to say sounds like aesthetic finger pointing, do what only you can do: Bend my finger back on itself until it hurts, and don't let up until I say, "Lord, is it I?" I mean it.

Dear Savior, even the most poetically gifted hymn writers strain when it comes to expressing your person and attributes. And the Scriptures themselves—soaringly magnificent, commanded by you and given divinely guided voice by a host of writers—fall short, simply because human language, even that bearing your Word, is not you. If we are tempted to think it is, cleanse us from this subtle kind of idolatry.

I realize that very average people often take up pen and say something about you, often poorly. But Lord, you know the difference between those who strain to do the best they can, and those who are not as good as they think and don't much care. You also know about those who collapse your greatness into a shallow assortment of adjectives and a few other common-stock words, then repeat, and repeat, and repeat, eyes cast ceiling-ward, standards non-existent, all connected to the ultimate sign-off: "It's what's in the heart that counts."

You have been brought down too small by these shenanigans, Lord. And irony of ironies, most of this glibness is found among the very ones who should avoid it like the plague: the new "worship music" folks whose professed task is to "lift you up, to exalt you," and to mine the riches of the Holy of Holies. It seems as if very few care about depth, great poetry, theological richness, Psalms, Job, the Song of Songs; care little more about the compact writing of Paul, and outside of Scripture, the Wesleys, Martin Luther, Isaac Watts, and countless honored word wrestlers and truth champions.

Lord, please remember the first sentence of this prayer, and bring it to naught if it doesn't matter to you. But if two thousand years of heart-and-mind searching, profound simplicity and simple profundity, great preaching, masterful exegesis, passionate theology, and Word-searching hymnody have any Kingdom meaning, please stop this pileup of lyrical fluff and theological froufrou. Cramp the wrists of the ever-so-ready writers and jack-leg theologians. And if they persist, keep them at home singing in the shower.

Lord, in your mercy, cleanse the singing church, even as you did the temple.

29

Concerning your testimonies, I have known from old that you have founded them forever. The entirety of your word is truth. And every one of your righteous judgments endures forever.

—Psalm 119:152,160

D EAR LORD,
It's beginning to matter less and less to me that scholars do this, that, and the other thing, trying to explain your Word. I'm not as shook up as I used to be when I hear of redaction criticism, cutting, splicing, deutero-this and tritero-that, or for that matter, Bible-believing dispensationalism. Please understand, Lord, I'm not defending just anything that anybody does to your Word. I think much of it is wrong, clever-headed, arrogant, and antiseptically clinical. A lot of it is debatable, and some if it is so nit-picky, it reminds me of someone trying to dismantle a battleship with tweezers.

Here's what counts: No matter what is done with your Word, it's still your Word—all of it. And it's refreshing to know that so many of these differing and differentiating *savants* care about the Bible so much that they can't let go of it; they can't let up on their fascination with every word of it; they can't quit thinking about the way God has revealed himself. They are reverent; they love God; they have profound insights into things that many of us conservatives are afraid to think about for fear of being ostracized or falling off the edge of the straight and narrow. They imagine, they laud, they worship, they conjecture, they put their foot down, they raise their eyes to heaven, and, to a person they are amazed at your grace and mercy, dumbstruck by your glory. And many of them have a sense of sin that would make D.L. Moody envious. They're Reformed, they're Roman Catholic, they're Anglican, they're mainline, they're sacramentalists; they long for baptisimal water without worrying about its place in the conversion sequence. They want to confess Jesus as Lord and proclaim the singularity of living by faith.

So here's what else counts, dear overseeing Lord: After all's said and done, when the debates die down and coffee and bagels are served, when the variously complex doctrines of the Lord's Table are turned to baby talk in the disturbing presence of bread and wine; when the Creator God, the Saving Christ, the Spirit-Breath are the talk of the table; when the conjecture, contumely, and counter-option surrender to these eternal wonders, then everyone is drawn back the Word, your Word, O God. They *must* call it that because it *is* that, and no amount of rethinking, de-mythologizing, and re-mythologizing can undo the simple glory of God having spoken, and hearts having been strangely warmed and turned toward the unique Son of God.

And who are these folks who steal away to your Word? Whom do we find? Why, the religious left, right, and center. We find scholar and tinker, doubters and shouters. And, drinking deep, lost in the fullness of the Wine of Heaven and the Bread of Life, they seem to have no time for squabble, no time to look up to see a dissenter or contravener or a fundamentalist or liberal next to them. For they drink of one Wine, one Lord, and one Way. This cannot be disputed. They might come away with different reports, just as those few did on Easter Sunday. But while there, they drink, they eat, they are filled and are slowly fitting into Christ's prayer for oneness.

I join them, for I, too, must steal away to your Word; sometimes barely able to crawl, sometimes out of breath trying to get there before the accuser does. But when I venture there, and venture on the One who is always there, I am fed with whole food. I feast on the manna, the True Manna, the Living Christ, for whom no theologian (or company of them), no interpreters or re-interpreters, can suffice. But strangely, I find something useful in what each dissenter has tried to say, but without the dissension. I find that I can tuck all these scholarly somethings away in my hungry heart, for use here or there or everywhere. I find this Word of God to be so rich and manifoldly nuanced, so beyond religion and so far ahead—beyond and above the Baptists, the Presbyterians, the Anglicans, the Roman Catholics, and the Charismatics; so imaginative and full of coordinated surprise; I find one emphasis here and another there; in another place I see them coming together in strange completions. And if I'm not careful, I might leap too quickly to one emphasis before it weaves itself into others, and drop into narrow doctrine-shaping instead of waiting for the divine whole to subsume the parts. And here's the joy, dear Author: I soon find that everything is about the same thing and the same One, and in finding this and him, I find peace and harmony because I keep seeing the Lord.

So, Lord of the disagreements, let a thousand of them bloom if you wish, but watch over them, please. And give each of us the intercessory perseverance and peace to wait on you, to pester you for your unifying touch. Take charge of each debate; tend each one with your water and your Spirit; prune each one with your truth-tools; uproot any alien graft; take joy in the perfume of the harvest. And then, O Lord, calm down our craven attempts to do your gardening. For this is your business; you are the vine and we are the branches; this is your pasture and we are your sheep. Thank you for going out, whip in one hand cleansing the Temple, staff in the other gathering your sheep, seeing that not a one of them is lost.

Amen.

30

And being in agony, He prayed more earnestly. Then His sweat became like great drops of blood falling down to the ground.

LUKE 22:44

Behold and see if there is any sorrow like my sorrow . . .

—LAMENTATIONS 1:12B

DEAR SAVING CHRIST,
 I want to guess at something the Scriptures don't come right out and say. And, even if my guess does not please you, the truth surrounding it will outshine any side trip I might be disposed to take.

Dearest Jesus, nobody really knows when you became sin. Some believe it to have happened when you were nailed down and brutally thrust up. Others think it began when you said your soul was "exceedingly sorrowful, even unto death." Then in Gethsemane the final weight came crushing down and sin was cast *upon* you, but it wasn't until you cried out in eternal forsakenness that it became one *with* you. Even though these things are shrouded within your counsel, the fact is clear: you became sin and bore our sins away.

But the thought that won't leave me alone seems embedded in the very facts that comprise our salvation, even though I can't locate a scriptural fact for it. The thought is this: I believe that you shed your blood effectively, not once but twice, and the first shedding guaranteed the second and final one. You were in Gethsemane—bent low and troubled beyond thought, praying again and then again about the possibility of release—when, in the anguish of this struggle, your body began to tear itself apart and your sweat became a confusion of blood and water. As you finally acceded to the will of your Father, and (may I guess again?) as angels and archangels—your sworn lieges—had to be held back by the Father from swarming over the edges of glory to fight for you; as

65

these darkest of moments compressed into a single hell, the blood and water flowed as a sign that you yourself had avoided the frightful sin of turning from the will of your Father. Once again, in the garden, as in the wilderness, you triumphed over the supreme temptation. Once again the preemptive strike was yours and yours alone. The victory you gained in Gethsemane was heroic beyond words; it took your blood—not redeeming blood, but resisting blood—and it sealed your crucifixion. And, could it be that the writer to the Hebrews had something like this in mind when he reminded us that we had not yet striven against sin to the shedding of blood? Maybe so.

As a result, you went to the cross already a victor, but still the victim. And there, having become sin itself, you shed your blood again; omnipotently this time, for the divinely appointed reason, without any response from the Triune One with whose reason you had agreed from the eternities. And then, you—the victim, victorious in forsakenness, befuddled, trashed—were turned to nothing, the ages-long work of Satan. This time, yes, this time and for all time, you took away the sins of the world, every last one.

When we think of what you endured in Gethsemane and on the cross, it's no wonder Isaiah had to write about you the way he did. Yes, beautiful Savior, fairer than the meadows, you were once disfigured and marred beyond belief. The first blows were struck—not from the soldiers and the crowds, the spittle and the thorns, but within your own body— from the working of your will within yourself. And from the time the disciples fled your ugliness, to your cry of forsakenness, when even the Father had to turn away from you, there was this repulsive something about you that nobody—nobody—could stomach.

But once you said "It is finished," and once you gave permission to your last breath—may I imagine again?—did not some kind of beauty, even the slightest inkling of it, cross your blessed features? You had done your work; the sins of the world were erased, you were sin no more, the east and the west had conspired to distance the curse from us all. And, when you were being wrapped in the swaddling clothes of this final, stony manger, did not your Father reach down and smooth your face a little here and there, just like a grieving wife would—giving that final touch to a wisp of her loved-one's hair, so it would look like it used to? If music had been played when you were laid to rest, would it not have been more like a slow and sobered dance—a sarabande, or a lullaby? I think so, and so did the great worshiping craftsman Sebastian Bach in the closing music of the St. Matthew and St. John Passions.

Dear Jesus, I have imagined this way only because I love you, only because the story of your gift to us all is limitless in its scope. I don't want to play fast and loose with Truth; I have no desire to add to it or detract from it. I want only to search within its riches, and offer something acceptable to you that is dear to me. Please remember that I've done nothing to question the revealed truth of that crushing Friday, or the evolving glory of Sunday next. I just want to say, "Sir, I would see Jesus in as many ways as possible!"

And before the time comes when my faith is turned to the sight of you, I want to find more and more ways to think you through and to thank you. So, maybe I can best end this prayer by asking *how* I can thank you, just as one of your children did when he penned these words: "What language shall I borrow to thank Thee, dearest Friend; for this Thy dying sorrow, Thy pity without end?" But even in my asking, knowing my tendency to buy my thanks by impressing you, I hesitate. Maybe Christina Rossetti had the secret when she both asked and answered a similar question:

> "What can I give him, poor as I am?
> If I were a Shepherd, I would bring a lamb;
> If I were a wise man, I would do my part;
> Yet what I can I give him: give my heart."[2]

Yes, that's what I'll do: I'll give you my heart, Lord Jesus, using again and again these asking-words I was taught to sing as a little boy:

> "Into my heart; into my heart;
> Come into to my heart, Lord Jesus.
> Come in today; come in to stay;
> Come into my heart, Lord Jesus."

Not that you would ever leave, dear Lord; I just love to keep asking.

---

2. Christina Rossetti, "In the Bleak Midwinter," stanza five. She wrote this poem in 1872 in response to a request from *Scribner's Monthly* for a Christmas poem.

31

Therefore the Lord also has highly exalted Him and given Him the name which is above every name, that at the name of Jesus every knee should bow, of those in heaven, and of those on earth, and of those under the earth.

—PHILIPPIANS 2:9–10

DEAR LORD GOD,
        Let this prayer about your Son consume my thinking, even if it means spending the rest of my life dwelling on each of these unfinished sentences, one by one:

Jesus above all.

This Jesus, the Lord Christ:

The Unique Son of God.

The Only Savior.

The Lord of all.

The One by whom all things were created and in whom all things consist.

The One in whom are hidden all the treasures of wisdom and knowledge.

The One who found it a lovely thing to take flesh to himself, joining the unlovely, working among them uncounted works of love, without restraint, without condition, without end.

The One who, in the face of the most severe temptation, showed us that Adam and Eve need not have sinned.

The One who, during his thirty-three years among us, worshiped the Father unceasingly, did his complete will untiringly, and summed up all the promises of God in an incarnate and eternal Yes and Amen.

The King who was lowly born, lived among the poor without once coveting, lived among the wanton without once lusting, and walked among the doubting without once tainting his faith.

The One stricken, scarred, and scorned—nothing to be desired of him—yet in whom the beauty of holiness shone unblemished.

The One who, in the isolated horror of bearing the sins of the world, suffered massive punishment so that we need not suffer the same.

The One—forsaken by the Father, homeless within time for an eternity—who, in a burst of perfect faith, hope, and love, took firm hold of his Father: "MY God, Why...?"

The crucified One who took a thief to heaven with him.

The One now risen, victorious: death and sin broken, unable to hold him.

The One still bearing scars but now emblazoned on an eternally perfect body—the promise of the bodies to be someday ours.

The King of kings, born in a manger, suckled by a virgin, Emmanuel, God With Us; among our garlanded trees, Lord of the gifts beneath them; the everlasting theme of the feasts, the carols, the rhapsodies, the dances.

This is our Friend Jesus, the Lord's Christ, the Groom, the Host, the Guest, the Great Physician, the Welcoming One, the Living Stone, the Supreme Shepherd, the Shelter in a storm, the Manna in our desert, the Bread of Life, the Wine of Heaven.

Alleluia! Alleluia! Alleluia!

32

And there are also many other things that Jesus did, which if they were written one by one, I suppose that even the world itself could not contain the books that could be written.

—JOHN 21:25

DEAR BETRAYED AND FAITHFUL Lord,

Tucked away in St. Mark's account of your betrayal, there's mention of an anonymous youth who, only partially clad, had been following you. He was seized, and in breaking free, lost his shirt and ran off naked. Nothing more is heard of him, and aside from a tradition that says it might have been Mark himself, nobody knows who it was.

Once again, dear Lord, I'm asking that you'll allow me to imagine an alternative. It might not be accurate, but there's nothing in it that would be contrary to you and your work. What if it went this way: What if this kid was one of a bunch of gangbangers—homeless, roving, marauding—who had been drawn to you? Maybe you had found a way to connect with them: teaching them, visiting with them, sharing bread and fish (leftovers from that huge picnic we read of elsewhere?), and slowly winning them away from the hurt and crassness bred out of homelessness, hatred, and overblown macho. There they were—the bottommost layer of the unmentionables, despised even among the gluttons and sinners from whom the righteous kept their distance but who you so lovingly visited.

And in those times when you went away alone to pray, did you really stay alone the whole time, or was there some kind of signal you gave these rogues that said, "I'll be on so-and-so mountain come sundown. It'll be just us, no crabby and cramping priests, no cynics and intellectuals, no politicians or merchants, no sheriff, just us. And we'll pick up on the rest of the good Samaritan story, and I'll show you how it might well come your turn to wipe the blood off a tax collector, or a Pharisee, or someone like him whose house was broken into, whose wife and children were scared silly, and who got beat up big time trying to defend them. And remember, this guy might just have been the one who foreclosed on your parents and ran them out of town."

Dear Jesus, it wouldn't surprise me one whit if it turned out that you mixed with some very dangerous people, maybe even before you made your first public appearance. It wouldn't surprise me one whit if you had hidden ministries that had to remain that way, unknown even to the Evangelists who so faithfully tried to report on everything you did. You—who harrowed hell, victorious in death—could just as easily have harrowed the underworld, or whatever it was called, back when you knew the street. How many gangs—or whatever they were called back then—came to softness and kindness because you knew where they were and went to them unafraid, piercing them with love and breaking their bravado with quiet authority?

Today, dear Jesus, today—right now—in one city after another, street kids and gangs hate, pester, molest, kill, rape, and rob. They're feared and hated, and most of us want them strung up by their tender parts. But do you? I think not. How many of us are willing to take a higher road, pleading with you, taking no rest and giving you no rest, until you break in all by yourself with the weapons of convicting love and sure-fire truth; until these fearsome and pathetic waifs, these mother's children, these images of God, are reborn into the likeness of the very same Savior who may have visited their brothers two thousand years ago?

Dear Christ, I'm not asking the impossible. I'm asking for something that is easier for you, much easier—if I might quote you—than getting the upper crust and the self-righteous through the eye of a needle. I'm asking you to remake these kids. Remake them and then return them to the streets, broken-hearted now, eager and ruddy-cheeked, as your witnesses. Show this torpid, prayer-sleepy church that all by yourself you can turn a whole layer of humankind right side up. Embarrass the wise acres who have written off the power of the Gospel. Wake up the soldiers of the cross who have limited the battleground to the safe side of fallenness. God, at all costs, come hard after us and teach us to pray until our throats go dry, and our hearts need a sabbath. And beyond our prayers, raise up a cadre of street evangelists whose path follows hard after the one I believe you took long ago. Raise up a streetful of kids who will follow you, even to the loss of the shirts off their backs, long after the rest of us have forsaken you and fled.

Lord, in your mercy, hear this prayer, and may it only be a start. Amen.

33

O God, You are more awesome than Your holy places.

—Psalm 68:35

Dear overlooked Creator:

My brother-in-law has a piece of shrapnel that was removed from his dad's hip in World War I. It's real to him, almost as if he had been there himself. I, too, have held it in my hands and been taken back to the pain, the splintered trees, and crimsoned trenches of that useless war.

But it's a trifle.

I was in Leipzig once, and worshiped in St. Thomas Church where old Sebastian Bach worked. I went across the street to the Bach Library and saw his manuscripts under glass; I saw his personal Bible, marked up and thumb-worn. I was even able to procure (legally, mind) a fragment of stone from the church itself. The feel of it; the smell of altar wine, old wood, and prayer books; the nearness of his handwriting—it's as if a couple of centuries surrendered their hold and let me in with him, and with Luther, for that matter, who preached a Pentecost sermon from the very same pulpit that I touched. On another trip to Germany, I visited Wittenberg Cathedral. The exterior was being renovated, just as with St. Thomas Church. I took a chunk of stone from a dumpster out behind the building, and with it visited that irascible reformer in my heart.

Ephemeral, this.

I also own a piece of the Berlin Wall, and a smooth black stone from Dachau. I look at the fragments from St. Thomas and Wittenberg. I hold them together with the Berlin Wall fragment and the Dachau stone. I see the Cross towering over the wrecks of time and the sins of the world, and rejoice in an eventual victory, not yet full won. These have a certain, affective presence, dear Lord.

But these, too, are trifles, Lord, ephemera.

I found a piece of a Japanese fighter plane when I was in Papua New Guinea some years ago; I went to Bloody Ridge in Guadalcanal and found two or three spent thirty caliber cartridges under the ashes of a recent grass fire; I saw the tower at Henderson field, and gun emplacements—touchable they are—on Red Beach. World War II, a romantic distance—some forty years' worth—from a young kid, Harold Best, playing army out in the field with his peachy-faced buddies, suddenly brought tears and reverence all at once.

One time, my parents took me to Mount Vernon, and I stood goose-bumped and awe-struck just a few feet away from George Washington's tomb, having read that his body was preserved well enough to be recognizable. Those few feet of distance dissolved and my imagination's eye saw inside. Could anything haunt me more? Not ghost-haunt, but hero-haunt. To this day, six-plus decades later, I can recall the combined weight of fame and fable pressing in as I stood there, a pubescent hero-worshiper in knickers, shirt, and tie.

Lord, I've read about those who would thin their bankrolls for a lock of a superstar's hair, a Mickey Mantle autograph, a mint-condition muscle car, a Picasso. These, too, are mere baubles. But, dear Lord, how powerful they are. How they take a hold on us, consume us.

But compared to what? To whom? To you, O Lord? To your presence? Your grand and reverberating handiwork? O Father, how often you fade in the company of the ephemera; how easily you fade. How often our faith-eyes give way to our earth-eyes, for we can touch what we see; we can own it, show it off. It's always physically there, and you're not.

Dear God, dear overlooked Creator, here I am, caught up in the midst of everything around me, no particle of which would have been possible without you. Everything, every, every single thing, is of your creatorhood, whether a pine needle or a cell phone. None of it would be here without you. Your touch is everywhere; your imagination outruns the Bachs, the Vermeers, the Hubbles, the Plancks. They have no music to make, nothing to say or study or report, without your prior mind having thought first, without your prior hand having shaped, your eternal Son having said Yes and Amen to it all, and without your generosity in allowing us to use your handiwork—for that's literally all we have—to make our own things. And beyond these wonders—infinitely beyond them—you yourself are here, right now, ready for the eyes of faith to open wide to the startle, the glory, the everlasting love.

I know Lord, once and a while when we quiet down, a God-thrill pushes at us. Now and then we have honest moments of hush; occasionally we blurt out: "When I behold the wonder . . . who am I?" And in the rare times when our faith does come alive, and your mercy shelters us from the barrage of questions you posed to Job—when the massive glory of I AM THAT I AM takes us down—in those times, when we own up to our withered hosannas and mealy-mouthed hallelujahs, your grace and mercy reach down to say that you do hear us. With the little attention we pay you and the nominal credit we give you, you still persist in your patience; you wait patiently while we sleep through your glory and slog our way from one evidence to another, awaiting something that fits our definition of big, some kind of sign that *really* shows your power, or calling some tawdry convenience "a miracle"—O dear Lord, have mercy.

Open our eyes lest we sleep the sleep of death; lest our enemies—especially our self-created, friendly ones—triumph over us. Don't laugh us to scorn. Don't take the eyes of faith from us; instead enliven them and bring them to sharpened focus. Awaken us to the perpetual shock of being among all your stupendous works, from a field daisy to the empty tomb. Be sure, dear Lord, that your Holy Spirit persists with us; that he will so quicken us that the merest twinkle of dew, the slightest breeze, a bowl of soup, a mother's smile, will awaken us and keep us awake, widely awake, worshipfully awake. Take us away from depending on the earth-bound thrill of ephemera.

Then Father, in our work, in the bread-and butter grind, in the hourly rhythms and routines for which you give us skill and strength, in the ways we think and imagine—cause us to walk alongside you in supplication and humble dependence. Let us seek the mind of Christ; let us remember what he said about Solomon's glory and the treasure of a tiny field flower. Holding this comparison dear, we ask that your work will be the real work we cherish, the real, everlasting wonder, and that our work will be humbly quieted and faithfully offered. Then, Lord, maybe we can be assured that touching your garment, or hearing your Word, or smelling some rosemary will turn our worship away from an autographed baseball or a lock of hair.

34

The Lord is not slack concerning His promise, as some count slackness . . .
not willing that any should perish but that all should come to repentance
. . . consider that the longsuffering of our Lord is salvation. You therefore,
beloved . . . beware lest you fall from your own steadfastness, being led
away with the error of the wicked.

—2 Peter 3:9, 15a, 17

Dear Sovereign Lord:
How long does it take for you to answer a prayer? Most of us want you to respond right away. And most of us assume that the result spells the difference between whether you've actually answered, or chosen to remain silent. If you accede, you have answered; if you don't, you haven't. This is wrong. Taking no for an answer from you is still an honor.

Or, if we took the ancient prophet's prayer for the peace of Jerusalem for an example, would we say that you won't answer at all, you haven't answered yet, you've answered another way, or you've denied the request? If we look ahead to Christ's towering high priestly prayer, especially his words about the oneness of all believers captured within the oneness of the triune God,[3] what or when is your answer, given the endless disunity within the Bride of Christ? Is it a "no" answer, a "not yet" answer, or a "yes" answer that we keep overlooking? And why do we thrill over the hymn-words, "We are one in the Spirit, we are one in the Lord," as if we were really, honestly living them out while sequestered in our various sectarian and theological safe houses?

What about Christ's prayer on the cross, when he asked you to forgive everyone who crucified him, because, according to him, no one had any idea of what they were doing? Was he praying only for the mob that railed at him, or was he praying for every last soul from Eden forward? We believe that the entire human race, in Adam, crucified the Savior.

3. John 17:20–24.

Doesn't this mean that each of us was included in this prayer? If so, can we come to terms with the disturbing implications? Did you ignore this universal petition because Christ had lost his efficacy in prayer by becoming sin? If so, how could his words to the repentant thief have any merit? Is this a symbolic prayer—a simple matter of exaggeration— within which are hidden the "real facts" about forgiveness to a foreordained group? If so, what words of Christ can be trusted? Did you in fact forgive them/us all? If not, what does that say about the efficacy of Christ as Advocate? How can somebody be forgiven without confessing? If crucifying God is the single most evil thing a person can do, are all lesser sins forgiven because of Christ's prayer? If so, then why not come right out and say that everyone will be saved because it all happened at the cross when Christ's praying and his atoning blood came together, and the sins of the whole world were taken up and dissolved?

Where does that leave us? At odds with the doctrines of eternal life and eternal punishment? Are the latter softened, requalified, reinterpreted, because of your Son's praying? Is this another way by which some say the Scripture eats away at itself, or we eat away at Scripture? Or, in this one simple prayer from our Savior, is there something of such profundity that it harmonizes all the seeming theological quandaries, and puts every human being on notice—from the sternest followers of predestination, to the on-again-off-again free will champions, to the most benign universalists?

Yes, Lord, it does. This prayer contains a double truth. It not only widens the atoning work of Christ beyond our most fervent longings, but it contains the possibility of the black-on-black horror of eternal lostness. The words, "for they don't know what they are doing," hold the key; words that imply what more than one apostle calls "ignorance." If there are those who when they sin don't know what they're doing in more than the usual sense, there must be some who do know what they're doing, likewise beyond the usual sense. If there is such a condition as profound ignorance, there must be one of profound knowing, because, dear Lord, if the issue settles on ignorance in the usual sense, or knowing in the usual sense, then everyone will be saved, or no one will. Those who crucified Christ certainly knew what they were doing in the usual sense, but our Savior saw beyond this and radically redefined "not knowing." Even in his anguish, as he suffered untold indignity at the hands of those around him, he set the conditions that distinguish the usual from the ultimate.

Lord, I pray that I'm thinking straight, but it seems that sinning in ignorance can include one or more possibilities: 1) not knowing or barely knowing at all; 2) knowing nominally, or superficially, but not understanding the depth and full import of what I'm doing; 3) understanding the depth, but not acting on it—sinning in the face of understanding. The second possibility seems to describe the work of the crucifying crowd, and the third describes the likes of Peter, when he denied knowing the one whom he had earlier called the Son of the Living God. And it describes me and, I suppose, most of us Christians—certainly our obstreperous friend, Martin Luther, who regularly confessed his sinning as knowing full well what he was doing.

Maybe, Lord, ignorance is an entirely personal matter, and every individual is responsible for sorting out the difference between not knowing, knowing but not understanding, or understanding but not acting on. But then, Lord, I am afraid for myself, because my sins—from years past until right now—have been committed somewhere in that murky color shift from not knowing, to knowing and not acting on; for all the while that I've sinned and still sin, I know Jesus to be the Son of God; I know the exceeding sinfulness of sin; I know and I sin. Where am I in all of this?

So, Lord, given the enormity of your grace; and knowing the extent to which you went to forgive, from Adam on, even the entire crucifying world; I think there must be a portion of humanity—an evil remnant headed up by Satan himself—that fully knows what it's doing, and, in a fullness of knowing that goes beyond anything that can be called ignorance in any of its forms, persists in crucifying Christ—rejecting him and everything about him, in the fullness of their knowing and in the very center of heaven-sent Light. Dear Lord, is this the difference between sinning ignorantly in its several shades, and mining the depths of the sinfulness of sin itself to such a degree that Jesus himself is repented of?

I hope I'm correct, and that this hope is not simply temporal hope or quantitative hope, for then I would be, of all people, most miserable. But this hope is in the Lord: it is fixed in him, given full energy by him, and fueled by all of the comforting words that have flown the eerie distance from his mouth to my aching and hungry heart.

O Lamb of God, I pray that your mercy, so bountifully extended to this ignoring world, will break stony hearts, and will kindle a flame in the cold dark of even those who are in the Light and stand ready to turn it full-off forever. I ask you to shut down ignorance in all its forms. Lighten our eyes lest we sleep the sleep of death.

Dear Jesus, break in on this world. Clarify to each of its citizens this one single thing: *who you really are*. Bring full Light to false light and then, by your convicting Spirit, cause everyone to see the difference, repent of their ignorance, and kneel at the feet of the only Lord, the only Redeemer, and the only Hope. Instead of allowing us to worry about who's saved and who's not, instead of witnessing about you as if we were peddling fire insurance, help us to do the one thing that Jesus commands us: To go into all the world and preach *Good* News, the news of light unto light, faith unto faith, hope unto hope, and love unto love. Help us to live this way, witness this way, pray this way, worship this way, and die this way.

Amen.

35

". . . you have left your first love . . .you have there those who hold the doctrine of Baalam . . . I know the blasphemy of those who say they are Jews and are not . . . you also have those who hold the doctrine of the Nicolaitans . . . you allow that woman Jezebel who calls herself a prophetess to teach and seduce my servants . . . . I know your works, that you have a name that you are alive, but you are dead . . . . I know your works that you are neither cold nor hot . . . you say 'I am rich, have become wealthy'. . .and do not know that you are wretched, miserable, poor, blind, and naked . . ."

—REVELATION 2:4B, 9B,14B, 20B; 3:1B,15A,

DEAR LORD OF THE Bride the Church,

Reading church history is not a very pleasant experience. You know that not a few have given up on you because of the messes, the heresies, the internecine persecutions, the divisions, the breakaways, the ousters, the false comforts, the contradicting applications of your word, the suspicions, the witch-hunts, the adulterations.

Yet, you are building your church. And, in the words of your Son, the gates of hell will not win over it. And this promise, patient God, comes alongside your Son's plea for unity, in his high priestly prayer. And neither the promise nor the prayer seem quite answered.

But glory of all glories, your self-assurance, your own confidence in the way you do all things, your willingness to look the fool to a cynical world and a doubting and shifting church, your willingness to keep working on your own terms and according to your sworn testimonies both puzzles and cheers us. After all, Lord, not one of us can look at the bleak side of church history without understanding our own personal role in it. We don't read about the prophets jumping on the relevance train, adjusting their message and getting with it because they were losing their audiences; we don't see your Son getting nervous when people fell away right and left. He just kept on, fully confident of the truth.

Somehow you don't adjust or re-invent. You just keep repeating yourself, knowing that your word is sure and secure within your counsel. Save us, please, from our shopworn and superficial attempts at relevance; forgive us from trying to keep up with the cultural Joneses and the itchy church-hoppers.

For if there is any encouragement in our history, and any evidence for your persevering ways, it lies in the very *existence and persistence* of this battered, tattered, victorious Church. Because outside of your plan and without your continued oversight, your Church would have disappeared long ago—maybe not too long after the fire of Pentecost was turned into the daily grind of church growth. Dear Father, there is no religious system under the sun that can lay claim to a God who is Love himself, unconditionally and perseveringly: a self-sacrificing God whose forgiveness knows no bounds. No religion can lay claim to anyone like the Son of God, this single, triune Redeemer, who—through thick and thin, light and dark, war and peace, confederation and dissembling—stands ready, towers above: our King, Sin Bearer, Servant, open-armed Ready One, and ever-patient Lord of lords. God! How we underestimate him—this triune Redeemer and his soldiering humility. Help us to love him all the more, looking less to the messes and more to the throne, down hard on our knees and rising up eager to talk about him. Please help.

Dear Lord, it seems that if we had paid more attention to a consistent practice on the part of the prophets, the apostles, and above all, the Son of God, we would be far more unified than we now are. In spite of their anger, outspokenness, and sometimes odd behavior, they held on to this axiom: Keep fighting and keep joining *at the same time.* Lord, nowhere do we read of the prophets wanting to separate and go out and start their own thing. Nowhere do we read of them doing anything but preaching hard against evil, spiritual harlotry, and social injustice, and then, in the name of the Everlasting Redeemer, inviting the wayward back home; back where the persevering chose to remain.

This seems odd in the face of our denominational breakaways, our urge to separate over one kind of malpractice or another. We have disagreements about the millennium, the amount and meaning of the baptismal waters, the issue of sanctification, the combined puzzles of free will and your sovereignty—and Lord, even right now, full in our face, the murky, puzzling matters of sexual orientation. Dear Lord, it seems that breaking away, purging the body, and trying to start up with a cleaner slate is the only way to go. Yet, we haven't learned that when we break away and form a new group, we multiply the chances for the same to happen again and again.

Lord, you know that today there might be more breakaways than ever before, many of them over deeply contentious issues, others over minor doctrinal whims, and even some over following a pastor to his next digs because he has convinced his mesmerized flock that his way is Jahweh. Give us strength to see even the worst trials through as a unified, organically linked body. We are a Bride after all, not a set of brides or contending bridesmaids. Lord, you won't divorce us, so why do we divorce each other? Come down hard on us, Savior. Bring an iron fist if necessary, but please don't take your Holy Spirit from us. And above all, help us to understand that being wounded but united is far more like Jesus himself, than being separated and provincially smug. Amen.

36

. . . For the mouth of the Lord has spoken.

—ISAIAH 1:20B

"Is not My word like a fire?" says the Lord, "And like a hammer that breaks the rock in pieces?"

JEREMIAH 23:29

DEAR OUTSPOKEN FATHER,

Thank you for the entire Bible. Thank you for entrusting yourself to those who, trusting you in turn, wrestled into writing what you wanted to say. Thank you for talking about everything from lilies to hog slop to eternal life. Thank you for choosing all kinds of people to write; thank you for allowing their personhood to show, even while yours overshadows each. Thank you for the best story telling ever; for the wild width of Psalms; for the sweet, uncle-like, love-drenched circle-sentences of John's epistles; for the relentless scope of Paul's work. Thank you for telling us about your creation-work in the old beginning and the beginning yet-to-come, in such a way as to lead us to, and keep us with, the Savior. And forgive us right here and now for making such an unwarranted interpretational mess out of each story, for trying to make the old beginning into a science project, and the new beginning into a lock-step timeline. Thank you for allowing things to be said that are wrong, and thank you for correcting them. Thank you for saying the few things necessary for our salvation in a thousand ways. Thank you for brief, pungent, wisdom statements; for some pretty convoluted, even unfinished, sentences. Thank you for humbling your counsel and clothing your wisdom in words themselves; thank you for being unafraid of our misuse of words—unafraid of our carelessness with them, even as you have used our words to speak unchanging Truth.

Thank you for knitting deftly together so many ideas, conditions, and kinds of people that single, unshakeable truths are offered us in mere sentences; all the while wrapping everything around the person of your Son, in whom all treasures of wisdom and knowledge are found.

No matter how variously we talk about your word—preach from it, distort it, reorganize and harmonize it, paraphrase it, take it through the mills of higher criticism and Christ-centered scholarship; even though we wish that you would have been a little more, well, *organized* about its contents (a little more like the way our cherished Long Range Plans are written: all compact, step-by-step and loaded with sequential problem-solving); even though some of St. Paul's sentences are longer than this one is—the lovely fact remains sealed up in this age-worn call and response: "The Word of the Lord." "Thanks be to God."

For the Bible *is* your Word. All of it is somehow your words—all you needed to say. No single one of us, and no cadre of moral and intellectual virtuosos on their own could have doped out our common plight and its resolution so firmly, variously, resonantly, finally, lovingly, humanly, comprehensively, and humbly as you did. And to top it off, your very own Son, your Christ and our saving Lord, summed the whole of it up perfectly, quickly, and unequivocally in word and deed: he brought to light what the ages could not erase and the detractors try to darken; he clarified what the prophets were straining to see; he brought the whole of the law and prophets down to two simple and saving commandments; his words tower above all other words. This Word cannot be shaken by scribal errors, redaction criticism, tattered manuscripts, questions of authorship, lost and missing fragments, problems in dating, vague verbs, unknown nouns and adjectives, distorted syntax—not one whit of the confusion created by sincere, skeptical, and doubting scholars can undo the simple glories of Christ's Godhood, his birth, life, death, atonement, resurrection, saving power, and eternal lordship. That we have this Book at all—this God-breathed treasure in the earthen vessels of sinful writers and undulating words—is beyond any earth-born imagining.

Dear Author and Finisher of your own kind of freedom, help us to quit yammering about the fine print we have turned into "orthodoxy." Keep us from tripping each other up over interpretations which, when it comes right down to it, we wouldn't and shouldn't die for. Bring us to the place where living for you is as simple, direct, unequivocal, and final as the martyrdom that might come of it. Amen.

37

"I have not spoken in secret, in a dark place of the earth . . . I, the Lord, speak righteousness, I declare things that are right."

—ISAIAH 45:19

Lord God,

May I talk about your word another way? You know that I believe all of Scripture is of your making; that it cannot be divided, subtracted from, or added to. Even though some books within this one Book are thought to disclose more gospel and doctrinal "meat" than others, even though opinions about this vary from time to time and person to person, in this prayer I want to thank you for inspiring one very strange and disturbing book in particular: Hosea. Thank you for taking on the brazen and shameless sinning of your chosen people the way you did. Thank you for insisting on your steadfast love, and vividly and frankly declaring it in those few pages. Lord, there is nothing in all of Scripture that comes close to what you did in this book. You have so weighted it down with the imagery of scandal and disgrace as to come dangerously near contradicting your own commandments. Were not you yourself, most holy Lord, the main character; were not you, in your everlasting love, sovereign over all possible subjects; were not the final plea about everlasting love crying out for a return of purity, then this book might be seen as a wrong-tune counter melody to the Song of Songs.

Who else but you would take this risk and command Hosea to do the very things against which your Law stands firm? Here you are, God, telling one of your saints to marry a whore; to have children by her. And later on, when she is shown to live both as a whore and an adulteress, you tell this longsuffering prophet to marry her again. Who else but you would ask a man to do this unless you saw yourself in the same plight: married to this harlot Israel, somehow knowing her whoredom long before you chose her to bear your name; staying married to her, even though in her marriage she added to her whoredom by committing adultery; renewing your marriage vows time after time. Who but you could see this through to the end? Who but you could emerge the victor, pure and unsullied; you, whose Son became sin in order to destroy it? Did you somehow become sin here, as a foretaste of what your Son endured, or is this stretching things a bit? I don't know the answer, but I do know that at the risk of going against your word you stayed true to it, by showing us that everlasting love covers a mountain of wrongdoing.

This book tells the truth in more telling ways than anything in the entire canon. Who cares whether this account is history or parable? Either way, within it you commit yourself to things that take us way beyond the moral conventions that you yourself established—you command unequal yoking, and you seem to fly in the face of your own Son's words that anybody who marries after divorce commits adultery. You even go so far as to say that you will stay married to the one with whom you are unequally yoked; that by implication, you are willing to risk adultery to win this whoring bride back to fidelity and purity.

God, for those of us who have long lived numbly, dumbly, disinterestedly, and sloppily—repenting and backsliding, repenting again and backsliding once more, then once more, then once more . . . . For those of us who have been finally awakened, and have found reason to struggle with forgiveness—wondering if you've grown tired of our meanderings, our unenlivened orthodoxy, our shameful procrastination—for the likes of us, this grand and scandalous book comes like sweet spring water where once there was pollution and muck. Over and over again it pleads for return; it promises healing; it even mentions backsliding—in the plural! Think of it! Thank you! It leaves no penitent out; it overlooks no one who is broken and ashamed. It calls back the whole whoring world; it pleads with the wandering, wavering church, the Israel of God; it is the beginning word and the final word. It is Gethsemane, Cross and Gospel, all in one scandalous story. It is unassailable. It is the cosmic "whosoever will" that finds a thousand voices throughout Scripture. It is God himself, at dusk, out looking for Adam and Eve; and from that time on it is the Almighty Creator, pure and holy, love unabashed, dying and crucified, serenading his creation.

O dear Lord, thank you. Thank you for going to such lengths to assure the most wretched and whoring soul that there is a Redeemer: mistreated, scandalized, and rejected, but Redeemer nonetheless. Thank you that in this simple sentence he said it all: "Him that comes to me I shall in no wise cast out." Thank you for the flood of promises that give their own account of undying love. And thank you just once more for Hosea. Amen.

38

For we do not wrestle against flesh and blood, but against principalities,
against powers, against the rulers of the darkness of this age, against
spiritual hosts of wickedness in the heavenly places.

—EPHESIANS 6:12

OGOD,
Why is there so much fear in such a love-laden thing as Christianity? Is it because bad news is preached before good news? Is it because the wrong sins, the measurable ones, are so easily repeated and inventoried, their sum nearly insurmountable? (After all, something like pride only happens once, and though it's a lifetime sin, it doesn't seem to add up the same way.) Is it because "accepting Christ" is loaded down with so much detail and stepwise motion that one wonders if all the bases can ever be covered? Is it because we have turned simple Abrahamic faith into an impossible glossary of faith-like attitudes and feelings?

Or is it Satan himself? Dear Lord, help us to understand that Christianity is the only life that truly frightens him; from his corner he attacks and attacks and attacks again. He twists and re-twists Truth. He encumbers it. He accuses with it. He understands all too well that other religions are idolatries, friendly to his designs and enclosed in changeless dark. He and his cohorts need not bother with them all that much, except to give continual assurance: aiding and abetting them in their various inversions, assuring them that they are on the right path. But not so Christianity: its very nature is Christ himself, the King of kings and Lord of lords; its very author is the One who threw this pretender from glory and saw him fall like lightning from the heavens. Satan's only God is the one true God whom he hates, whose lordship he cannot abide, whose truth he reverses, and in whose prison he will be eternally chained.

But until he is taken down, he stays nasty. Wrapped in false light, he'll do anything to make bad things look good and good things look bad. He'll do anything to turn joy into sadness and assurance into doubt.

87

He is clever-stupid enough to speak against his very nature by telling Christians that they are lost and hopeless. He laughs while he lies, acting in complete blasphemy, as if it were the Lord himself convicting us of unforgivable sin. He manipulates Scripture so as to keep it at odds with itself. He knows how to frighten us—as he did venerable old John Bunyan—with Hebrews 6 and 10, with Esau's weeping. He makes us think that we are the only exception to John 6:37 because it doesn't mention our name, and because "I will in no wise cast out" might have some dark alley behind the "no wise." And he sees to it that if God loves Jacob and hates Esau, we are Esau and the real saints are the Jacobs.[4] Dear precious Savior, he did this to me for years and I concluded—you know this well—that I would spend eternity in hell loving you with all of my heart. The dark he imposed on me was horrifying, and, despite a few Sabbath's worth of respite here and there, he had me pinned down. And even now, forty-some years later, he still tries; but you know how much I've been captured by your love, how enormous and far-reaching Christ's saving work has come to fill my heart. You know, dearest Lord, how I'm learning that faith is not a sense or a feeling, but a truth-driven decision based on nothing less than your thousands of promises.

I'm learning to rest in these sweet, distilled songs of Scripture. I've also learned the danger of returning over and over again to just a few open-arms-forgiveness "key" verses, for this is not how your Word works. Key verses do not always unlock, but your entire Word does. The whole of it, in its enormous sweep, is about repeated sin, one Savior, and infinite grace. I have come to see that a great part of our difficulty with you is not over what you say about yourself, but what we *think* you say and how we *feel*. Dear Lord, I ask that you narrow my hearing to the expanse of your own voice. Let me listen to you singing your solo: triune counterpoint in one everlasting melody—at once a serenade, a lullaby, and a grand march—absent the accompaniment of over-zealous helpers, explainers, and whereas-ers.

Dear Savior, these words come hard, not because I'm ashamed to repeat them, but because they might sound self-serving. You know that I believe in engaging with Truth itself, and I resist "me-too" praying and "let's-trade-experiences" talk, but perhaps there are others who are going through what I did and need to know that they are not alone; that they are not the one damned exception. And I want to walk with these

4. Romans 9:13 quoting Malachi 1: 2–3.

ones—these disciples who love you unashamedly, who are intoxicated with your Word, who have no trouble in speaking about your infinite love to the worst of other people, even though they have difficulty applying this witness to themselves.

O Lord, deliver them this instant; cast Satan away as far as the east is from the west, and faster than lightning falls from heaven. Grant your peace, and flood every doubting and fearing soul with Jesus himself, who has promised never to cast anyone—not any single solitary one— out. And as one of your great missionary servants once said, "These are the words of a gentleman."

In Jesus' name, please.

39

"Lord, how often shall . . . I forgive?"

—MATTHEW 18:21

ALMIGHTY GOD,
How many times have we blown our estimates of you? On what small amount of knowledge are our estimates based? We think we have your infinity pegged and then discover that we have to move the pegs. So, we keep this up, peg leapfrogging peg, and sometimes we move the pegs backward because something has come up that shaves you down a bit. We glorify you when we get a closer look at a galaxy and then, when a nine-year-old boy—yes, this is really the case in my extended family—comes down with glaucoma and faces the possibility of blindness, our estimates shift. Somehow, we have failed to see you completely in all of your actions, and in everything you allow without actually willing everything—or do you?

Lord, it might be better if we threw away all estimates of you that are based on our ways of measuring greatness and magnitude: size, shape, volume, length, distance, time, quantity, extent. Even though you told Abraham that his progeny would outnumber the sands on the shore; even though the heat of this or that yonder star is known to be a thousand thousand times that of our sun; even though our sins can't be counted (by us, that is); we should not respond by saying, "God is bigger than all of this." As soon as we do, we change your size to outmatch our various totals and we're back to estimating.

We are always estimating, measuring, even though we sing songs and write books about infinite this, that, or the other thing. But back behind this—that is, back where we live, move, and have our being, clockbound and number-struck—we still count on you according to the way we have counted you up.

Why do I say this? Am I fair in saying we all do this instead of saying I alone do this? Whatever the answer, it still involves counting, and

90

it is counting from which I beg release; because counting and estimating seem to love each other's company, just as adding and subtracting and multiplying and totaling are incomplete without each other. Why am I praying this way? Why do I waste my time and yours (there, I'm counting again), hurting because I can't fit this massive thing called existence into your instant endlessness, this massive thing called sin into your grace, this massive thing called universal holocaust into your love? Why is my blessing bag smaller than my curse bag (There, I'm counting again.)?

God, I run to your Son. We run to your Son. He alone of the Godhead was sent down among the counters and estimators—nine months in the womb, weighing such and such, growing how many feet tall, thirty years and then three more, forty days and forty nights, five thousand loaves, so many gallons of new Cana wine, where are the other nine?, seventy times seven, ninety-nine plus one sheep—numbers, numbers, numbers. But I run to him because he outran all the numbers. He outlived the numberers: "Lord, exactly who is my neighbor?" "Lord, I've kept all the commandments from my youth up." "How do you expect to rebuild the temple in three days?" "How many times should I forgive my neighbor?" "How long will it be before you establish the Kingdom?" "This widow married seven times, now whose wife will she be in the resurrection?"—and so on, dear Jesus, we continue to be lost in numbers.

Dear Christ, dear Alpha and Omega, Author and Finisher—all of these all at once, no limit, no starting gate, no finish line—please see to our pathetic sense of capacity. Don't make it bigger—no more bean counting, please—don't even call it measureless because we'll try to out-size size just once more. Take us where faith, hope, and love are. Cause us to make our everlasting abode there and there only. Take us to the substance that faith *is*, and away from the substance that that we try to convert *into* faith. Take us to what hope *is* and away from what we *hope* it is. Take us beyond what love *does* to what love *is*—God Himself. Take us to these places; better yet, take us to this three-in-one-in-three place where abiding and Abider are indivisible.

Deliver us please, at all costs, from the tiniest tendency to plus-and-minus you and your work, and take us into the transfigured air of complete trust, vigorous testimony, and unqualified stewardship. Amen.

40

I will open my mouth in a parable; I will utter dark sayings of old.

—PSALM 78:2

L ORD,
      O how I love to read psalms, if for no other reason than the way they skip around from one thing to another. This is the way I pray. I can't get things in a row, and Jimmy's broken arm jumps in as I thank you for a bright morning and marmalade on toast. And while I'm deep in prayer over a lost world, I begin to flounder in something I heard on CNN—something about obesity or health care. Perhaps not all psalms are this disjointed, but they do comfort me in the wonderful bump that one request gets from another.

Then what? I read some scholarship on Psalms and find out that many of these bumps and lumps may have come from this or that scribe splicing this or that in; from an eager editor, or from a fragment disappearing, or a long-lost verb staying lost, with contextual guesswork replacing translation. And then I think, well I'm a lousy pray-er after all, and all the support I thought I was getting from these passionate and disjunctive writings are simply matters of flawed put-togethers and textual criticism.

So what, Lord? Let's assume the critics are right and the "original" was one gorgeous gem of architecture, shining like a cut diamond. But then, what about the scribes and clerks? Were they smoking something, or were they such a collection of under-gifted dolts as to emend so awkwardly? Or—hear me now—had they actually fixed up an even rougher piece of praying—something more like the way I bang and bump around when I pray? Why not? Did they turn out to improve things rather than crazy-quilt them? What is the daily prayer of Everyman like? Is it an attempt at literary genius or a record of the human soul facing the scatterings of circumstance? And is Psalms the most telling collection of both? The critics seem to have overlooked this possibility, but I in my praying have not.

And they can overlook the way I pray as well, and spend time reflecting on the way *they* pray. Meanwhile, I can return to these wonderful chunks of everyday outpouring: these rushes of praise, this let's-get-even talk, this lament and protest. I can read the discursive dead ends, the lashings-out and the gatherings-in. I can say, Thank you, mighty Author, for causing such bumptious talk to be found in Holy Writ, and then allowing it to become its hymnbook. Thank you, dear Foreseer, for looking around and ahead into the mountains of human pleading and praising, and then assigning your Son the eternal task of placing each syllable at your feet with a force, clarity, and delicacy that no one of us deserves; no, not even King Solomon or Lancelot Andrewes or George Herbert or Jonathon Edwards.

So, dear Author, thank you again and again. Let the scholarship come and let it go. I thank you for it, but no longer will I let it jostle me as to how I ought to pray. O! that there were three hundred of these psalms instead of half that. And then a thousand more. And without presuming to displace them, I'll keep kneeling alongside and trusting the great Advocate to do the editing, even as I take comfort in the most perfect prayer ever, the one your Son taught to his floundering disciples: *Our Father in heaven, hallowed be Your name. Your kingdom come. Your will be done on earth as it is in heaven. Give us this day our daily bread. And forgive us our debts, as we forgive our debtors. And do not lead us into temptation, but deliver us from the evil one. For Yours is the kingdom and the power and the glory forever. Amen.*

41

The law of the Lord is perfect . . . . The testimony of the Lord is sure . . . .
The statutes of the Lord are right . . . . The commandment of the Lord
is pure . . . .

—PSALM 19:7–8

DEAR GOD,
How does anyone pack the eternities and launch into one of
the most important books in human language with a half sentence? How
does anyone collapse the promise of salvation into a dozen words without a verb? Your servant St. Mark did.[5]

Who could write another book, and somewhere near the middle
get so blissfully entangled with the richness of the gospel and the joy
of circumstance that for some 140 words he pushes on without really
finishing the sentence, then bumps it up against a parenthetical byway,
and eventually brings it all down to a sort of safe landing, only to launch
into another 120-word sentence? Your servant St. Paul did.[6]

What collection of books could tear so frankly into the complexi-
ties of earthly circumstance, and end with the bliss of an eternal home,
with such abruptness, patience, urgency, frankness, frightfulness, horror, peace, joy, authority, assurance, and victory? Your Word does.

Who but your Holy Spirit could oversee all this traffic? Who but
your Son, the Word made flesh, could bring it down to a life of purity
based on a mere two laws on which the whole of the Law and Prophets
are safely hung?[7] Who but the Triune God could bring himself from
eternity to time, from speechless Speech to nouns and verbs, from unim-
peded joy and glory to connivers and killers, from the beauty of holiness
to the grime of fallenness? You did. You do. You'll still do, until you once
more say, "It is enough!" And then St. Mark's half sentence, St. Paul's

5. Mark 1:1.

6. Ephesians 3:1–12.

7. Matthew 22:36–40.

over-packed luggage, and the entire counsel of God-made Scripture will take wing and soar to the eternities, where you and everything about you are All in All; where there is no Temple, because *you* are the Temple; no Bible, because *you* are Word; no theology, because we will know even as we're known; no more exegesis, because *you* are your own explanation; where Alpha and Omega dissolve—three words are too many and not enough.

Dear God, assist us; no! push us; no! thrust us; no and no again! Personally take us; yes, take us there yourself, into the might and power of every word of your Word. Bring your Holy Spirit into the fray, for he's the only One who can take those sixty-six bolts of many-colored and variously-textured cloth and make them into one lovely, iridescent garment, woven from top to bottom without seam. Please undo every effort from me, from others, from the evil one, to make of your Word what you never intended: a contrived patchwork, at odds with itself, hesitant and unsure.

We trust you for this, dear Author and Finisher, dear Word made Flesh, dear Comforter. For you alone have the words of life and we have no one else to turn to. So, let the half sentences declare themselves: make them swift and sure as darts; unwind the long ones: let them flow like a mighty river; stand in the middle of every utterance: straddle the extremes and close the breaches made by false prophets and arrogant counsel. Bring us around, time after time, to your thundering confidences and your quiet solace. Unstop our ears, unlock our voices, give sight to our eyes and strength to our feet, as we follow hard after the One who walks beside us.

Amen.

42

My son [my daughter], if your heart is wise, my heart will rejoice—
indeed, I myself; yes my innermost being will rejoice
when you speak right things.

—PROVERBS 23:15–16

DEAR MASTER:
Thank you for clear-eyed, purpose-faced, confident young people. Thank you for putting that something in them that assures us older folks you have not given up on leadership. Thank you that charisma is more than the narrow, shifty thing many Christians have made it out to be. Thank you that something can burn in the very young that makes us want to listen, even to follow them. After all, even a little child can lead us, or is your Word mistaken?

Thank you for those parents who know that someone has been born into their home whose gifts may show ever so early and outrun theirs. Thank you for humbling them, for quieting them as you did Mary when she simply tucked certain things in her heart and pondered them. Lord, if these parents are tempted to gloat, to push, to primp and idolize these youngsters—take hold of them and remind them that you have done this work of which they are simply stewards. Give them wisdom, then; wrap it in thanksgiving and cover it with meekness and grace. Let these gifts bring softness and moral health to their offspring. At all times, bring understanding to intelligence and servanthood to purpose.

Lord, you know better than anyone how easy it is for gift and purpose to be turned sour, to be directed self-ward, to be grafted into perversion and ravage. You know how thin the line is between loving and worshiping oneself. You know that the final degradation of charisma is narcissism, and you know how cleverly the narcissists can conceal the evil and dress it up as light. You know where they are, what damage they are doing, and how they will ultimately implode on themselves. You know that the urge to say, "I will be like the Most High," is not Satan's alone, but ours. You know how the spoken desire to "serve others" is all too often a cover for serving ourselves, and you know that being gifted is not the same as being good.

And then, Lord, because these young folks know no other culture than this present one, where entertainment and narcissism are fused together, deep-rooted, and even Church-wide; because this seems so natural to them, Lord, to whom can they turn even if they felt the need? Please intervene, Great Physician; bring your Spirit to bear. Purge the body of Christ, especially its local leaders, artists, and lead pastors. Bring unprecedented otherness, humility, meekness, and brokenness to their giftedness. Burn out any trace of self-centeredness. Raise up Christ-centered mentors everywhere: in the home, in the workplace, in the schools; if necessary, bring the whole of the entertainment world to an embarrassed and slobbering halt; make its idols into stuttering, lisping shells. But redeem them, please.

Visit these purpose-driven kids with your Spirit and your truth, however and from whomever these may come. Turn the light of your gospel directly on the hearts, minds, and wills of the gifted. Bring them to the Savior, whose salvation brings sanctification to giftedness, whose Spirit is life itself, and whose way is servanthood. Teach them the very same thing that Christ learned: that what they've been given is not something to be grasped or clutched, but given away. Teach them the way of emptiness that they might be filled, and in turn, give their fullness to the fallen, the empty-handed and poorly-hearted, the widow, the orphan, the beaten-down and diseased. And above all, while they serve, keep them from doing good things merely from civil righteousness. Give them Jesus himself, in whose Name and for whose glory they stoop, lead, serve, and worship.

And then, O Lord, since you made most of the world average, show us that we, too, can fall into our own versions of self-worship. Sanctify our ordinary dignity; don't let us worry or fret when more attention goes the way of the gifted. And when we are ripped with jealousy because we are not the center-stage leaders, cause us to think on a certain Carpenter ages ago; help us to understand that if he was made like most of us, he must have been average, too. For how could God have allowed a genius to be Messiah? Wouldn't that cause us to think that only special people can do what he did? Wouldn't that furnish us with another excuse for not taking the role of a servant, and a blue-collar one at that? No, it shouldn't. But it can show us what average people can do with their hearts and minds when they are completely given over to you, the Fount of all wisdom and servanthood.

Dear Lord, my daughter often says this: "God is very good at his job." And since you are, and since you decided on the spread of giftedness within the human race, teach every citizen, from the nuclear physicists to the stevedores and nannies, that they have but one kind of work to do: to love you, to love neighbor, to love themselves, to love doing your will, and to worship you in humbled service, bathed in the very love of which you are the essence.

Amen.

43

Then the Lord God called to Adam and said to him, "Where are you?"

—GENESIS 3:9

"For the Son of Man has come to seek and to save . . . "

—LUKE 19:10

D EAR GOD,
Again I come to your overwhelming work in the creation in
Genesis, in Psalms, and especially in those thundering creation questions you posed to Job. In all cases, they proclaim your creating might,
laud your vast imagination, and paint pictures of inestimable beauty,
majesty, even charm. But they do not quite take account of the explo-
sive, destructive, and cataclysmic forces within creation; from way out
among the galaxies down to our earthly habitat. My mind jumps to the
endless holocausts that continue to mark the ways of humankind—
genocide, starvation, filth and disease, AIDS at an international level,
plagues, totalitarianism, persecutions, and terrorism. In a similar way, I
get caught up in the history of the wayward church: its inquisitional sins,
the Crusades, heresies, burnings at the stake, witch trials, doctrinal wars,
even confusion among many as to which narrow way is the right way.
On top of this, Jesus talked about things getting worse and worse, about
the many who would be lost and the very few who might be saved. And
here's the real puzzler: In the face of this, he told us to keep spreading the
Good News as if the saved-lost imbalance didn't exist.

Then comes another question—a Psalms question, but from a
different angle: What—who—are we that you should take mind of us?
What is there that's truly personal about you? I know this question has
been asked down through the ages, but I have always shelved it as an
example of those who don't really see into your grand purpose, those
who "just don't have faith." And I know about the flood of pedagogical,

99

doctrinal, and theological responses which attempt to harmonize the cosmic debacle under something like "final victory." But now I want to ask some questions, not out of a loss of faith, or even from lack of faith, but out of a grieving and sobered curiosity.

I ask myself: How can I keep nesting and resting within my personal faith when the world population is exploding right in front of me? How can I keep calm when "many are called but few are chosen" becomes all the more unsettling as babies are being born right and left, creating a ruthless kind of math about the many *not* being chosen? Do I have a right to be grieved, even angry about this, in that my doctrinal bag is filled to the full with apologetics, with hymnic guarantees like "God is Working His Purpose Out," with a rehearsal of "the peace that passes all understanding?" Is this the kind of peace that scoffs at understanding, the kind that bypasses these frightful prospects and all their forbidding facts? Or is it the kind of peace that reshapes understanding only to surpass it out of the sheer weight of your omniscience? I prefer to believe it is the latter, but still I ask, Why?

My current answer might be a feeble one to many, but to me it towers. I realize that the skeptics could blow it out of the water because—I admit this—there's a certain circular twist to it, a certain "if-that's-so-then-why-so?" cleverness that only faith can turn into straight wisdom.

So here's what I say, dear Lord—not that you really need a defense, but from my side of it I want to do more than sit by, wrapped up in my just-trust-God blanket: First, I realize how sinful I am, not sins-*full*, but *SIN*-full. I understand more and more that when I feel like taking somebody out in bumper-to-bumper traffic—not road rage yet, just in-my-heart-bang-crash video games; when I push ahead in one of a thousand ways, large and small, at the expense of someone or something dear; and—Lord, this is just the beginning—when I watch a movie, and right along with Clint Eastwood or Matt Damon I can't wait until the bad guys are punched out or strung up; when I want to take over and run ahead of the legal system and kill a murderer, or personally emasculate a rapist; when I sit my self-righteous self down in my recliner and feel just that much more ballsy when I see smash-mouth football, or hide cruelty behind laughter when I witness a verbal take-down; when I buy something I don't need, and by extension shorten the life span of a sweat-shop teenager in Indonesia; when I do these things and more, and then get my multiplication tables out, I begin to understand something frightening. I am participating in the cosmic holocaust. I may not sin like a Himmler or a Hussein, but I'm in their camp, because I could spin even more dangerously out of control were it not for the curious providences that have so far kept me. I realize that the inventories of sinning are made possible, because along with the Himmlers and Husseins, I'm *SIN*-full, and I've turned this way on my own; that observing all the large-scale rottenness from the vantage point of my so-so sinning is to miss the point. By nature, I participate in all of it. Sin equals sin, and in the light of your purity all sinning equals all sinning—no one-to-ten gradations here.

And then, I begin to see your personal interest in all of this in a strange new light. In your knowledge that any person, any group, any nation is capable of taking the world down to ashes, your grace is at work keeping things from becoming worse than they are. You will not allow this. Mercy upon mercy, you keep intervening. Common grace runs alongside, if not sometimes ahead, of special grace. You have not taken absolute revenge. The rains keep falling on the just and unjust, a peach still runs heavy with sweetness and nutriment, honey still brightens our eyes, a baby's breath is still like a fruit orchard, and the earth is kept safely and beautifully in its orbit. Despite the ways we trample your creation underfoot and spit on the image of God in each of ourselves; despite this, with Satan at the mixing board, you intervene; you show yourself to be intensely mindful of us by holding back the full force of sin itself. Thank you for being mindful of us this way. And help us to keep renewing our prayers for your continuing, creational mercies.

So, when the questions come back, haunting and taunting: Are you mindful of us? Do you have a personal interest in each of us?—tell us to ask of your Son. Tell us to ask about him. Tell us that your personal interest—no, that is too pagan—tell us that your love is such—your love for this wallowing, crashing cosmos—is such that you and your Son, by your Spirit, took up citizenship on this parched ground, becoming a census-number in the dusty, plodding population of peasantry and poverty.

Tell us again how he started from scratch, he and his family. How he worked his way into manhood, scratching out a livelihood, grieving the loss of his dad, suffering the disbelieving envy of his siblings, wondering about the carpenter down the street always underbidding a new job, and maybe even putting up with a slightly pushy mom. He showed us that

Adam didn't need to sin. He showed us that where spit and taunting and cursing abounded, humility and forgiveness abounded even more.

Personal interest on your part, God? There's more, and it's a Cross-full, overcoming sin-full. Here's a man who not only joined the sinning world but promised that its sins—all these evil holocausts, from my part in them to the whole wide world—all these holocausts—would be erased by his single-handed, love-ridden work on the cross that we flaunting sinners nailed him to. Here's a man—in whom there was no sin—becoming sin. Here's a man in whom sorrow and love were comingled with blood and water. Here's a man so eternally in love with us and with his Father that for an eternity-within-a-Friday, he lost his Father and underwent eternal punishment.

When I consider the work of our hands over and against the work of your hands?

Is there a personal God . . . ?

Ask of Jesus.

44

As Peter was coming in, Cornelius met him and fell down at his feet
and worshiped him. But Peter lifted him up, saying,
"Stand up; I myself am also a man."

—ACTS 10:25–26

DEAR FREELY-CHOOSING GOD,
   I wonder what Paul, Peter and Amos were like when they
were writing down your Word. Were they different, on a higher-than-
usual plane, steady and true? Did they actually know, word by word,
that something uncommon was guiding their thoughts? What were they
like when they were having lunch or talking with friends? Could it be
that, sinners though they were, they were so in love with you, so utterly
given over to your gospel, so committed to your Son that writing down
your very words was just one more way of living for you, of living in the
Spirit?

   What I'm asking has nothing to do with my conviction that all
Scripture is your Word, given by the Holy Spirit. Instead, I'm wondering if anyone in love with you, walking intently and intensely in your
presence, could have written your words without knowing anything
other than your abiding presence. Yes, the New Testament was written
by Apostles, but being chosen as an apostle was no different than Israel
being chosen—you simply began somewhere with someone, and, in all
cases, had to abide their sinning, correct them, and then smile when
they repented and continued walking with you.

   What's unique about your Word, then? Certainly not Paul, or Peter,
or Amos. There's nothing about them that could not have been found in
any number of their contemporaries. It might even be that there were
those around whose lives outshone theirs, whose devotion to you was
light years ahead. For instance, what about all the women who stayed
by your Son while the men ran off? What about Phillip, who so clearly
preached the gospel to the Ethiopian eunuch? Or Stephen, whose grasp

of your work was as firm and authoritative as anyone around him? And look at Peter, who not only continued to vacillate after Pentecost, but was harder on Ananias and Sapphira, and Simon the sorcerer, than your Son ever was on him. Yet you chose him, and that's sufficient.

Lord, here's what is unique about your Word: You are. Your Son is. Your Spirit is. The messengers? They're simply messengers. Without you, without your enabling Spirit, they're like the rest of us—human, everyday stewards; some plain, some brilliant, some outspoken, some mild, some scholars, some uneducated laborers.

Lord, I'm praying this way to keep me from mistaking Paul, or Peter, or Moses, or Apollos for super stars: raising them too high, forgetting their complete and utterly limited humanity, their day-by-day sweat, their ordinary bodies, and their irrelevance outside of your work in them for their sin, repentance, and stewardship. And above all, Lord, I ask your forgiveness for demeaning your Spirit by attending too much to them, or anybody today charged with delivering your Word. Your Word is yours and no one else's. It is you speaking to us, even as you humbly work with an array of individual messengers. And why not? It is you who, in the very first place, created unrepeatable individuality. Who better than the unique Revealer could stay firmly in charge, while allowing such diversity and variety? So, dear Lord, while coming to know Paul, Peter, and Amos as uniquely individual fellow humans, just as each of us is, I thank you for their consecration, and turn from admiring them to worshiping you: Author, Finisher, Revealer, Interpreter, enthroned above the greatest of saints, and inviting us into your exalted company and their redeemed ordinariness.

O the mystery of God himself: infinitely able to take dry bones, fallen flesh, and stony hearts, and turn them into living sacrifices—strong, lively and consecrated—ready to preach the Gospel and write it down so that word and deed—his Word, and the matchless deeds of his Incarnate Son—would never pass away. Dear Lord, help me to live so heartily for your glory that when I'm asked to say or write something about you, I'll find it a joyful thing to submit to your Spirit's leading, just as did the chosen few: from Moses, to David, to Amos, to Luke, to Paul.

Amen.

45

It is good for me that I have been afflicted,
that I may learn your statutes.

—Psalm 119; 71

Or do you despise the riches of His goodness . . . not knowing
that the goodness of God leads you to repentance?

—Romans 2:4

Dear God of all salvation,
To anyone who laughs at you, smile back and turn them to tears.

To anyone who scoffs at you, sing them the song of Bethlehem.

To anyone who doubts you, show them your scars and then take them to breakfast by the sea.

To anyone who scorns you, turn their knees to water and their innards to mush; then wash them clean and give them Spirit-muscle.

To anyone who ignores you, stalk them in their days, haunt their dreams at night, and show yourself lovely in the sunshine.

To anyone who crucifies you, turn their hammers into ploughshares.

To anyone who belittles you, put them to counting loaves and fishes, and lugging Cana wine around.

To anyone who makes commerce with your name, turn their gold to dross and make them poor in spirit.

To anyone hears your call but once, let the eternities re-echo it until they call for you.

To anyone who says there is no god, show them their foolishness then make them fools for your sake.

46

. . . And we beheld His glory, the glory as of the only begotten of the Father, full of grace and truth.

—JOHN 1:14B

DEAR SAVIOR,
One of the best sermons I ever heard came down to a simple question: "Dear Savior, what do you want us to do?" with an equally simple answer: "Wherever you are, whatever you do, just say something about Me."

Dear Lord Jesus, forgive us for leaving you out of our conversations until we work up a time to work you in. Forgive us for thinking that witness is a planned-for specialty; a particular, rote-way of unwrapping the Good News. Help us to be so naturally taken up with your presence and so inhabited by the very thought of you, that "saying something about you" is the continuing light that lightens and guides every word we utter. And then, when your name is mentioned and your love emblazons every topic, bring the fullness of the Gospel down with such urgency that hearts break, knees bend, and faith is born.

Meanwhile, O Christ, lead us to the study table. Lead us to the words that others have written when they want to say something about you. Assist us in taking the words to ourselves and graving them in our hearts, so that when we are alone with you they fill our prayers. Or, if the occasion arises when we are asked to say something about you in a more formal way, let words like these anoint the ears of those who listen in:

If I ascend to highest heights; if the Spirit brings Jesus to me in unaccountable brilliance, and the glass is wiped clear of the greater part of its darkness, *Jesus is fairer.*

If I am permitted to see what I can only call the beauty of Jesus in the saintliest saint, *Jesus is fairer.*

If I happen upon a grand doxology, in which the best of the poets inscribes with the best of his best, *Jesus is fairer.*

If I could but once speak with the tongues of men and of angels, filled with a rush of unqualified love, *Jesus is fairer, the fairest of ten thousand to my soul.*

If I could compress the beauties of all of God's handiwork into one transcendent handful, *Jesus is fairer.*

If, in another handful, I could combine Sebastian Bach, Michelangelo, Brahms, Vermeer, Rembrandt, a heaven full of angel voices, a world of newly born babies, a galaxy of weavers, potters, and sleight-of-toe ballerinas—if I could hold this handful to my hungry heart and be filled with its glory, *Jesus is fairer.*

And then, Lord, as we pore over the many words your saints have written about you, these come to mind:

His voice as the sound of the dulcimer sweet,
Is heard through the shadows of death.
The cedars of Lebanon bow at His feet;
The air is perfumed with his breath.

Love sits in His eyelids and scatters delight
Through all the bright regions on high.
Their faces the cherubim veil in his sight,
And tremble with fullness of joy.

His lips as a fountain of righteousness flow
That waters the garden of grace
From which their salvation the Gentiles shall know,
And bask in the smile of His face.

He looks and ten thousands of angels rejoice,
And myriads wait for His word;
He speaks and eternity filled with His voice,
Re-echoes the praise of their Lord.
    Joseph Swain

≈ ≈ ≈

The great Physician now is near,
The sympathizing Jesus.
He speaks the drooping heart to cheer—
Oh, hear the voice of Jesus.

His name dispels my guilt and fear,
No other name but Jesus;
Oh, how my soul delights to hear
The charming name of Jesus.

Sweetest name in seraph song,
Sweetest name on mortal tongue,
Sweetest carol ever sung—
Jesus, blessed Jesus.
   William Hunter

Jesus, the name that charms our fears,
That bids our sorrows cease;
Tis music in the sinner's ears,
Tis life and health and peace.
   Charles Wesley

O Jesus, Jesus, dearest Lord!
Forgive me if I say,
For very love, thy sacred name
A thousand times a day.

For Thou to me art all in all,
My honor and my wealth,
My heart's desire, my body's strength,
My soul's eternal health.
   Frederick W. Faber

I will arise and go to Jesus,
He will embrace me in His arms.
In the arms of my dear Savior
Oh! There are ten thousand charms.
   Anonymous

Jesus, priceless treasure,
Source of purest pleasure,
Truest friend to me.
   Johann Frank, tr. Catherine Winkworth

~ ~ ~

IESU[8]
Iesu is in my heart, his sacred name
Is deeply carved there: but th'other week
A great affliction broke the frame,
Ev'n all to pieces: which I went to seek:
And first I found the corner, where was I,
After, where ES, and next, where U was graved.
When I had got these parcels, instantly
I sat me down to spell them, and perceived
That to my broken heart he was *I ease you,*
                     And to my whole is IESU.
   George Herbert

8. In Latin, the letters I and J are interchangeable. Herbert uses I both as the first letter in our Lord's name and the personal pronoun I, hence the remarkable force and reverential cleverness of the last two lines.

47

And everyone who has this hope in Him purifies himself,
just as He is pure.

—I JOHN 3:3

DEAR SPOTLESS LORD,
I'm trying to get the idea of holiness in my head and in my heart. Whether I use my mind to think, or my heart to feel; whether I improve a bit, and strive for a thinking heart and a feeling mind, I persist in falling short of the fullness of this word.

Dear God, please remember that I'm praying. I realize that I'll never fully lay hold of the dazzling beauty and searing purity that mark your very being. Words fail here, as they surely must—for no human, no angelic being, can ever know what you are from the inside out. But this should not stop any one of us from searching our language, getting as far inside your Word as the Spirit will allow, and striving to know something of the kind of holiness without which not one of us will ever see you.

But given the promise that our faith in Christ, our desire to be washed clean, and our walk in the light together grant us—knowing that the eternally Holy one makes his dwelling within us; knowing even, that while we find him in us, we are found in him; knowing these things to be true—we can begin to understand something beyond words about this grand word.

We can begin to learn that holiness is not a comparative word; not a word for something good among other good things. It's the only word for its own uniqueness. And even when we study all the words that seem to sum themselves up in holiness: hunger for God, thirst for God, striving against sin; loving God and neighbor with heart, soul, mind, and might; righteousness, brotherly kindness, surrender, confession, humility, Christ-centeredness, and sanctification; when we find ourselves longing with all our hearts to share in each one of these conditions fully, there is something still beyond, yet near; elusive, yet promised.

Dear Lord, is it this? Perhaps holiness is not the sum of wonderful words; holiness is its own beginning and final condition. It, like love, is the "without which" God is not God; it is the "without which" we cannot see him. Holiness subordinates and sanctifies all other words and gathers them up into the purest completion. It sums up each one in the very purity that God Himself is. Holy *is* the Lord, not holy *does* the Lord. God, I know I'm stumbling around the truth—I can't say it right. Forgive me. I desire you beyond words and lists of words, as precious as each one is. I long to be *like* you, *like* your Son, *in* the Spirit. I hunger after this likeness, not because I am commanded to be holy, but because holy is the only way to be.

So whatever it may cost—I measure these five words carefully—*so whatever it may cost*, please take me to yourself in such a way that being like you, being found *in* you, is my only passion, even as I walk on this world—in it but not of it—doing all those things that my upward call in Christ Jesus demands. And perhaps, Lord, instead of the things of this world growing strangely dim, as one hymn writer has it, perhaps everything—the pain, the rot, the usual, the noble, the useless and the useful—will come into such sharp uncompromising focus that my every step and every act will be as if you yourself were seeing through me, making your plea through me. O Most Holy God, hear this prayer.

48

Who has complaints? Who has redness of eyes?

—PROVERBS 23:29

DEAR CHANGELESS LORD,

Strange how a quad-shot americano often clears up my attitude about your love and mercy. What faith seems slow to do, caffeine steps in with a lift into loveliness that, for an hour or so, puts things as right as rain. And here I am a believer who should know better.

But what about those who might be looking for you? They might tell it this way:

Drugs, nostrums, fixes, buzzes, rushes—they do help. And what caffeine can't fix, a pay raise can. What a pay raise can't fix, a new Camaro can; what a Camaro can't, the lottery can; what the lottery can't fix, the hard stuff can.

But we'll stick to caffeine. Yes, caffeine—we'll limit ourselves just to caffeine, that's how self-respecting we are. The safe side is our side, and we'll seek you out amongst the Is-ness of everything, and another quad-shot should take us to the cool side of Being. And if caffeine won't do it, then we'll seek our very *own* Is-ness; and what that can't do, maybe seeing you and us together in an oak tree might; and what that can't do, becoming one with all of nature might, and then we could even become one with a dolphin, or a nasturtium, and you a jack-in-the-pulpit!

O lord, still and all, where are *you*? *YOU*? Is there a YOU? We'll try spirituality; maybe we can sneak our caffeine while we get into zen and mantras, and what zen and mantras can't do, gauzy robes and midnight séances might; what gauzy robes and midnight séances can't do, a relationship group might; what a relationship group can't do, Match.com might; what Match.com can't do, somebody's wife might.

So now what's left? Let's try church. Church: what the rose window can't do, the worship might; what the worship can't do, the music might; what the music can't do the sermon might; what the sermon can't do, the caffeine might—they have a coffee break right after worship time. Cool, now we're back to caffeine.

With all this stuff that might do it but can't, maybe you're watching, maybe you're waiting, and maybe you'll even speak. And then here comes a humble, praying, trusting believer—we think that's what he's called—smack dab into our company, straight into the path of us poor, suckered, world-wrapped, god-hunting folks. From this believer-person, love, truth, honesty, and straightforwardness lead to some talk over lunch; where the talk does its work, friendships come about; where friendship does its work, a witness grows into being; where the witness grows into being, a hunger develops; where the hunger develops, new birth comes about; where new birth comes about, growth marks the way; where growth marks the way, Christ steps in; where Christ steps in, caffeine comes back, no longer just a buzz, but a simple pleasure surrendered to the Royal Wine of Heaven.

49

Hear my voice, O God, in my meditation . . .

—Psalm 64:1a

Dear Lord,
  Thank you for the wisps of praise that now and then stumble onto my tongue. They are feeble and they are fleeting, but there they are anyway. Dear Vine-keeper, you are especially good at growing things; not only that, you can grow things out of nothing.

With these things true, I wait on you to establish your infinite worth more urgently on my tongue. Grow the feeble syllables into outpourings. Create anew those words that pretend at praise, but are tainted with bluster and windiness. And most of all, where there is no praise at all—not even a stumbling syllable or a preceding breath—come by and create from this nothingness a torrent of laudation. Come by and pour rain on my parched tongue, give voice to my raspy throat, and heal my leathered lungs.

And when the merest thought of you crosses my mind, turn it into rich remembrance. And then cause a list of your names and your works to weave themselves into one long promise. Cause each name, each work, to be magnified. Forbid that any of them fade; cause them to shine glory on every circumstance. And as you bring your response to this prayer, I pledge that I will never allow the show of your glory to congeal into a private possession, a personal pleasure, shut away from those whose tongues are parched; hidden from those who long to hear someone say, "Why yes; yes, the Lord does visit; yes, freshening rain does come to other parched tongues."

Lord, why else would any of us ask for your visits—for bursting hearts and eager tongues—except to let everyone know, to tell Good News everywhere, to laud your name where it might not otherwise be heard, to pick up where the heralding angels left off on that wintry night in Bethlehem?

Please bring answer to this prayer only for your glory.
Amen.

50

For there must also be factions among you . . . Or did the word of God
come originally from you? Or was it you only that it reached?

—I CORINTHIANS 14:19A,36

L ORD,
Why have you allowed the Church to invent so many variables
about life-and-death matters? And why have you allowed these to be so
at odds with each other? Here we are: a world full of sinners. But also,
praise be to you, here we are: a community of newly born Christians.
We profess belief in one holy catholic and apostolic church. We believe
in the forgiveness of sins, and claim Jesus Christ to be the only Savior.
We call each other brother and sister. We have all kinds of statements
about togetherness, and ever so many definitions of ecumenism, some
restrictive and others radically open-armed. It seems that the choice of
what kind of Christianity we want is more up to us than to you. Or, put
another way, while we all claim your Word as the source of all truth, we
craft versions of it that both allow for variable opinions and condemn
each other's variations. We can decide whether being born again is a
startling event or an organic process; we can decide whether baptismal
waters themselves regenerate or are evidence of regeneration prior to
baptism. We talk variously about losing our salvation or being eternally
secure within it. We can decide exactly how literal the Bible is and test
our entire faith journey on the decision. Some of us actually say that
if we don't believe in a literal six-day creation, we have given up our
right to say that the Bible is the Word of God. And while some of these
decisions fly in the face of orthodoxy, most of them are sheltered within
it. So, this must mean that orthodoxy, in one way or another, is at odds
with itself.

And way up the intellectual ladder, the deep thinkers create contrasting and often combative theologies that mark boundaries for the
most crucial questions: the presence or absence of our capability to turn

to Christ outside of your choice of us; the real meaning of the sacrament; losing, keeping, or missing out on our salvation. They decide on this or that interpretation of Scripture; they swear to the veracity of your Word while finding within in it ways to defend or attack sexual orientation, the conditions for divorce and remarriage, women in positions of leadership and ministry, doctrines of the last times, mortal and venial sins, the sinlessness of Jesus' mother, the nature and place of sanctification, or the necessity, desirability, and legitimacy of tongues. Lord, there's more.

None of this would be so important, if Christianity were simply an invigorated round table discussion with not much to account for beyond the discussion itself. But eternity is at stake—it's that simple, and that's what we're taught—and when questions of right and wrong, sin and righteousness have so many different doors and windows, what do we do? Does something become wrong or right because a synod or a council or diocese or denomination says so? Who shuts and opens the doors and windows? And, for that matter, who can brag about designing them in the first place? For we know about the Ten Commandments and the two greatest commandments; in a certain respect, we can do a pretty good job of obeying them in some broad, mechanical way, as did the one who told your Son that he had kept them from his youth up, as did Saul of Tarsus who, in matters of the Law, declared himself blameless. It's when these great principles and laws are broken down into everyday protocols and decisions; it's when they are interpreted, by Roman Catholics or Quakers or Mennonites or Southern Baptists or Wesleyans or Christian Reformed or Eastern Orthodox, in such a way as to set eternal pathways in confusing directions.

If ultimacy has any meaning; if eternal things count eternally over passing things; if there is a heaven and a hell; if anyone in his or her right mind wants assurance about gaining the one and escaping the other, but cannot get a clear answer as to what to believe, or how to behave, in the meantime; if you, our Father—the embodiment of unwavering and pure-light holiness—know exactly what is right, what is wrong, what *sin* really is, and, therefore, how *sins* come about; if you make no bones about such matters, then why? Why? Why have you not stepped in long ago, at least to set things right about something as sobering as sin and no sin? Why do you not step in, right now, and rough us up until every one of our counsel matches yours?

Why have you allowed such behavior when you, by your very nature, are so unequivocal, so sovereignly unambiguous, so imperturbably decided, so powerful? How could *anyone* go to the very end of oneself, giving up one's only son to contumely, disgrace, and atoning death—no other way, no other plan, no other option? How could you be so majestically unilateral, so omnisciently single-minded, and then allow the Church to turn the Gospel into such a contentious and confusing market place? It wouldn't be so bad if the Gospel remained the Gospel, even when founded on all these contrasting ideas—but wouldn't that mean your stability is subject to our instability?

Could that be? Is it something like this after all? Do you simply tolerate, even encourage, variation? Does all or most of it meet your approval? Is there something which is hidden to us—a certain dimension to sin, or some strange wisdom in your grace, so unfathomably primary but completely consistent with your changelessness and holiness—that allows for our vagrant conditions? Do you adjust to these variations only because you know that most of them have been developed in your name and for your glory?

If so, then the scandal, the confusion, the sin, must lie elsewhere. If it doesn't lie in the interpretations themselves, then it must lie with the interpreters, in their exclusivist and separating attitudes *about and within* these variations. They become the real bother, the cancerous blight. Is this what the world laughs at? Is this what confuses the world, and turns its mind toward cynicism? Is it us at our judgmental worst and not our variations that so rob the Church of its witnessing power? If this is the case, and if you are more at peace with our variations than with our attitudes, please visit us swiftly with your refining fire, your unsearchable wisdom. Humble us into the kind of unity for which your Son so earnestly prayed. Almighty God, if this is our sin, then what kind of judgment is in store for the Church? Will it be a judgment that excuses the variations, then slashes and burns us to ashes for our world-damaging attitudes about them? And are we guilty of two kinds of worldliness: being of the world (the usual sin), and the more hideous sin which feeds the flames of the world's innate divisiveness with the fires of our own? Are there really two Laodicean churches—one lukewarm to your Son, and the other lukewarm to the way it confuses a lost world?

Dear God, do these pleadings make any sense to you? In voicing them I am filled with fear, even doubt, because things get shaky—I get shaky—whenever I step out of my safe, sectarian box and see all the other boxes—some safe and internally sound, others safe and externally suspicious. Lord, have mercy on that part of me that always wants to know why, and cries out for your attention. And, Lord, give shelter and strength to that part of me that goes wobbly when I can't locate the ideal; especially when you, the Eternal Ideal remain silent, and those whom you have called to yourself, fall short.

So, dear patient One, I'm down to a few things I believe with a growingly persevering heart—things I would be willing to give my life for—a very few things. And despite my love of reading theology, studying doctrine, trying to write down a few ideas of my own, and conversing with brother and sister, I settle myself as a weaned child on just three things from which I pray a life of increasing holiness and Christ-centeredness will emerge. They are simple, just as you are. And they can be put in any order. The first is a life lost in faith, hope, and love. The second is a continual flight to, and fervent study of, your Holy Word; yes, all of it, my only written rule for faith and practice. And the third is a reveling and resting in the Holy Trinity, in whom the alpha and omega of all necessary righteousness and holy living is found. And dead-center in the midst of the One whose only center and endlessness is his Triune Self, I see and am seen by Jesus, the Christ—my Christ—to whom I give myself, in whom my faith rests, whom I declare to be Lord, and in whose full work and person—life, death, resurrection and full Godhood—I treasure in my heart.

Dear Heavenly Father, hear these questions from a fearing, loving, embarrassed, and curious believer. Who else would receive these questions with a patient hearing and a healing response but you? Dear saving Master, put the whole of your Bride, with all of its exclusivities and fractures, safely within your redeeming arms. And despite the various entry gates we have constructed; despite the many variable measurements we have imposed on what your Son called the Narrow Way; despite the extremes of self-crafted doom and superficial bliss; show the Old Way where the good things are, and in your mercy cause us to walk in it. Show your interest with devastating grace and healing power.

Hear this prayer, quiet my questions, visit us all; straighten us out and bring us, your Son's Bride, to transcending unity.

In the only Savior's name, this I ask, Amen.

51

. . . you are inexcusable, O man, whoever you are . . .

—ROMANS 2:1A

L ORD,
I have just two sins to confess and I know only one way out
of them. Every imaginable enumeration collapses under the weight of
these two, and every imaginable thing is conquered in the way out.

Pride and Unbelief—self worship and false worship—these are
the twinned sources of my ruin. The first causes the second, and the
second feeds the first. They are the Adam-in-Eve, the Eve-in-Adam of
everything baseless about me. Even in confessing them I can be proud;
proud that I'm not as bad as I could be; proud that I am a step or two
removed from the really proud; proud of my mastery of the protocols
of confession; proud of the ways I have been able to sort through the
cul de sacs of worldliness while others haven't. Proud, proud I am, and
even in repeating this damned word I'm proud of my insight into it, and
proud that I have even concocted the chutzpah to tell others of my pride.
I've gotten so good at this I can give the impression I've been humbled
enough to covet only a few moments of my audience's attention out of
an hour's worth of windiness. I'm proud that my (my!) audiences talk
about *my* style and latch on to *my* inquiring mind, and talk of *me* as a
godly person. I'm even proud of the sentences that I am now writing,
imagining a company of on-lookers and in-listeners who are waiting to
purchase what would only sell you short if they saw into my inner self.

And then Lord, I think of the stud-lust, the whore-hunger that
Pride has—buying its way to consummation, siring every possible sin
against others and against myself; all these sins likewise in heat—sniffing
the wind, wanting a life-surge, getting it, birthing its children, each given
a different name, each lusting for a life of its own, each too proud to
acknowledge a common father and mother, yet sneaking up to them,
nursing greedily and finding newer strength to be themselves. Name the

sin and you've named the father. Name the sin and you've named the mother.

Unbelief: another stud-whore-sin, another inbred, inter-marrying family. But not me, Lord. I might doubt, but I don't *unbelieve*. Yet, as I say these words, I'm dodging any connection, reaching into the pride barrel and pulling out a mucky handful of Pride's children: dishonesty, doubt, arrogance, mistrust, hypocrisy, and idolatry—pride made into its own pantheon—all those sins that eat away at belief and wrap it in the crust of self-delusion. And if I dig into the unbelief barrel, I'd come up with similar muck: pride, arrogance, hypocrisy, lust, idolatry . . .

So, I see the two sins grotesquely joined, siamesed, and I don't know how to give them a common name. I just know that something gives them common life, and that behind this something is an eternally corrupt evil one, in whom pride and unbelief are absorbed in overwhelming narcissism with a thousand faces and one purpose: to breed, to multiply, to encourage us in our sin, and draw us away from the Father and our only Savior, the one Way out.

Dear Lord Jesus Christ, however I look at myself in the glaring light of your perfection, I see a sinner in this choking, nerve-numbing headlock called sin. And looking into this thing called sin, I see its exceeding sinfulness—consumed by itself and consuming everything in its path. I see the one-by-one sins, each hideous enough to destroy, each bearing the same family resemblance, each commonly begotten.

And God helping me, I break loose and flee. In my blinding sin, I see light and I run toward it. And if beaten to a pulp, unable to run, I crawl. If I have no strength to crawl, I call. I flee, I crawl from the incomprehensible crush and corrupting burden, and I call to the one Way out. For I have a Savior who knows about sin, because he became sin without sinning. He met every kind of sinner when he walked among us. But even more wondrous: he welcomes, he calls, he knocks, he goes out looking; he seeks, he serves, he embraces, he pleads; he welcomes, he re-welcomes, he welcomes again, he waits. And waits some more. He binds up—he smites, yes, but he heals. He repeats these wonders seventy times seven.

And once he and I are together in this new-birth way, I can do what the publican did—collapse all my sins into one cry: "Be merciful to me." Or I can parse the plea and confess many kinds of sin; I can prolong my grief and multiply my inventories of wrongdoing, but they all boil down to the hideous twosome: Pride and Unbelief. And the Lord's Christ—Oh! how I love that doubly sufficient name—the Lord's Christ will always take his eternal time to sort it all out. And even if my list is incomplete, or if I call lust envy, or envy jealousy, or immorality unrighteousness, he'll understand. He'll do the sorting, because from the eternities he had already understood that sin is not just sin itself, but a confusion about what it *is*—how it adds up, divides, subdivides, multiplies to false totals. His precious blood has not only seen to the sorting out and to sin-by-sin forgiveness but—blessed be his name—to the complete erasure of the whole.

An old gospel hymn goes something like this, dancing its way from dark to light: "In the sea of God's forgetfulness, that's good enough for me. Praise God, my sins are gone."

So, dear Jesus, I know two sins and one Way out. But, may I now suggest another two-and-one combination: one Way out and two results, everlasting praise and everlasting life. Amen.

52

And beginning at Moses and all the Prophets, He expounded to them in all the Scriptures the things concerning Himself.

—LUKE 24:27

DEAR GOD,

Who is not some kind of a historian? There are those who, by training and profession, are equipped to write history. And the best among them surely must understand that they are mere interpreters: reporting, yes; gathering and integrating, yes; summarizing, yes; seeking wisdom, yes. But they have no final answers, no all-absorbing overview, no ultimate lesson. To a certain extent they teach, sometimes profoundly, but never finally. The best of them are earthen vessels, unable to hide their limitations: waiting for yet another discovery, another document, another opinion to help them on their way toward a bettered insight. This waiting and the re-doing that comes of it are history's most important irony and the historian's most telling humiliation; the best of them are just like artists, creating continually paraphrased versions of the same tree. And it's the beauty of the paraphrase that counts, rather than the tree itself. And the difference between good and bad historians is the same as with artists: Some paint better than others.

And there are the rest of us: the amateur everyday-historians and recounters. Story tellers who have the past in our blood, in our memories, on the tips of our tongues, in our family trees, and our never-ending tales: no retellings ever alike, each one its own paraphrase, and each one growing out of a remembered truth that no one of us can actually pin down and say, "This is it. This is the real tree."

Except for you, Lord. History is something only you fully know. You are the chief Historian, because you can put every circumstance from everywhere together under just a few wonders: your eternally Triune Being; your creation of things, creatures, and people; our rebellion against you; your sworn purpose to love and redeem; your provision, from your very Self, of a Savior. And the rest, as they say, is history, and no account of it suffices without all of these few sheer facts overseeing the whole. That's why, Father, your Word—Incarnate and inscribed—is the only history worth learning. And it is to this history that all earth-bound historians are summoned, for if they ignore it, they are mere part-time reporters and limited thinkers. No, the Scriptures do not contain every detail from every time and place; no, they are not history the way a professional historian writes history; yes, they might contain parables, poems, hearsays, visions, and fantasies; no, some details do not match others; yes, manuscripts have been lost, nouns and verbs have changed meaning, and some of the noblest Apostles could not always agree on very crucial things.

But YES, you have folded this otherwise confusing mélange called the human story into one—just one—possibility; better yet, one reality. And smack in the middle of it, containing everything knowable, judgeable, and redeemable about past, present, and future—smack in the middle of all of this is Jesus the Christ, God's only Son, our Savior, the Word made flesh, in whom are stored up, sorted out, summarized, redeemed, and finalized everything in the entire story.

You, I say again, are the chief Historian and Jesus Christ is history's Chief Answer. There is hope here, dear God, because only you know, and it is to you alone that we turn or we are undone. And we cannot turn as mere interpreters of your interpretations, mere commentators on your comments, but as people of faith who trust your finality: people for whom most things are too high, too marvelous, too difficult; people who join yonder psalmist and compose and quiet their souls like a weaned child resting itself against its mother, becalmed, taking Sabbath, preparing for the next mystery, and rejoicing in the peace that passes all understanding.

Dear Father Historian and Mother Comforter, we come to you, we trust in you, we rest in you.

53

My soul longs, yes, even faints for the courts of the Lord; my heart and my flesh cry out for the living God.

—PSALM 84:2

DEAR LIVING STREAM,
My favorite pastor and long time co-worker, Bob Liljegren, told this story in one of his sermons.

When he was in a seminary preaching class, one of the students was about to deliver a homily based on Psalm 42. In his best voice, the young man began reading: "As the deer pants after the water brook, so pants . . . ." The professor cut him off mid-sentence and told him to start running around the classroom. He made him run, and run some more, until his lungs went searching for air. Then the professor said, "Now get back to the pulpit and start reading."

"As . . . . the . . . deer . . . . . pants . . . . . . after . . . . . the . . . " And so he read, urgently, out of breath, unable to bring a single phrase to smoothness. And he began to preach, but now with an almost primitive and animal sense of disquiet and desperation. He, at least for those few moments, was brought head on with what real spiritual thirst, what a breathless pursuit of God, might be like.

O Lord God, I've thought on this story many times. And just the other day, I told it to my wife and broke into tears as its significance pressed me down once again. But the tears came in *telling* the story—in being moved by the story itself. But this is what I might do reading a novel, or watching a movie. My relationship to you, dear Lord, has to be more than this. There is more to living for you than identifying with someone else's story. Yes, to a certain extent, the story challenges me to long for you with heart-bursting intensity. But what is a challenge without a surpassing response? It does no good to talk about how much I've been challenged—how inspiring or touching or moving a challenge is—without a response that turns the challenge on its ear.

Yes, Lord, I shed tears, but how much do tears mean all by themselves? Yes, Lord, I long to long after you, but all too often this longing is like planning in order to plan, unless I can come to understand the doubled urgency of what Jesus said to his disciples in Luke's account of the Last Supper: "With fervent desire have I desired to eat this Passover with you before I suffer." Dear Father, only your perfect Son could speak in this way: fervently desiring to desire. Only he could say these words without wasting words, without simply trying to impress his disciples with doubled-up rhetoric. Only he could see through the weakness and into the strength of language, and risking redundancy, turn words back on themselves, multiplying their meaning with unfailing intensity and longing.

Dear Father; dear outspoken, truth-speaking Spirit; bring me to the kind of fervent desire to desire that Jesus has. Bring me further in my longing for you than merely being moved by being moved. I'm finished with second-hand desire and copy-and-paste versions of longing. Please cause something to happen in my being that takes me directly *into* your very Being. If I am truly *in* Christ; if Christ is truly *in* me, then follow through and allow me—cause in me—the high privilege of longingly longing, fervently desiring to desire fervently, even as Christ himself did. Save me from this continual habit of simply agreeing with Scripture without living deep inside its very essence. Please do this.

And even if this means being born again as if for the first time, but this time completely given over to you, then I'll willingly forsake every testimony I've ever given about you in order to say, just once, with absolute purity and continuity of heart, "As pants the hart after the water brook, so pants my soul after you, O God."

And patient Savior, if there is some curious theology at work here about new birth, I know you know what I really mean. I know you can handle my ways of talking about my sojourn with you. I know that you do not just knock once, but over and over. And we both know that nearly as often as I've let you in, I've left you standing just inside the door without inviting you to take permanent and sovereign lodging. Forgive me, dear Savior. Please come in, all the way in; stay here with me; never leave.

I do love you. Amen

54

DEAR LORD,
    I truly believe that you are in charge of many of the ways I doubt. I thank you for lending nuance to my doubts, bringing them to sharp focus, showing me where to doubt, surrounding me with unseen light, and protecting me as I make my way to your clarifying Word. I can honestly say, dear Lord, that every doubt I've had has been or is being transformed in one way or another by you and the sweep of your Word. Sometimes, the transformation is enriched by a related doubt, a kind of tributary. But most of the time you keep the doubt narrowed down to its beginning dimensions, knowing me fully and pressing me with exactly the right weight, even increasing its vividness so as to make your responses clearer and brighter. I have come to cherish and trust your power to narrow or widen my doubts, because you know the power of your truth, because you know me. You know how much I can handle, and above all, you know that there is no doubt in me or in anyone else that can out-jump or outlast your clear light. You know when to release me from doubt, stabbing it dead with Truth, and offering peace and joy in its place—sometimes instantly, other times as gradually as glacier travel. And sometimes, you lead me to a Sabbath of thought where I can rest as a weaned child on your wisdom-breast. How can I thank you, Leader and Owner of my salvation?

So, as I continue to walk in the Way, I ask you to give me the kind of meat and milk that nourishes me, even if I don't like its taste. You know I would rather have quick, sugary, fattening faith-snacks—spiritual comfort food that helps me to grow plump in the Lord; Burger King sermons and Taco Time experience books. As I have often prayed, I want truly to pant after you, but not because I have gluttonized and grown so blubbery that taking one step in your direction brings me to my knees sucking wind. I want to be lean and well-conditioned, so used to running races and living under the protection of your promise that I can run and not be weary, walk and not faint.

I hope never to ask you to remove doubts for the simple convenience it might bring to my heart and mind, just as I would never ask you to bring light to your truth just so I can have some kind of Sunday happy face. Lord, keep your kind of dark and light in cahoots with each other. Both are the same to you, and in this I take courage. Keep me sinewy; help me to lose false spiritual weight that I might grow up into the stature and fullness of the Savior, who alone can prepare a table before me, smack dab in the presence of the enemy. And cause that table to be furnished with the savory meats of salvation and drenched in the Royal Wine of Heaven.

Amen.

55

He shall cover you with his feathers, and under His wings shall you take refuge . . . You shall not be afraid of the terror by night.

—PSALM 91:4A, 5A

DEAR UNSLEEPING ONE:

The other night, the middle of it, I awoke gripped in spiritual darkness. I was terribly afraid—feeling like I was being sucked down into myself; tempted as never before to think that I was personally designing my own eternal separation from you; my life in Christ ebbing away, maybe even undesirable. It seemed as if I was being stripped of any capacity to love or be loved. You seemed to be gone and I was tempted not to care. I could only cry out in silence against this compressing, smothering, down-swirling evil.

I reached for my wife; she turned to me in her sleep and, as is often the case, began holding me close, tight close. I held her in response, a hopeless hugging at first; she hugged back and we simply lay there—snug, warm, knit close, hugging back and forth, she half asleep, her night breath warm and sweet, and I being slowly loved back from this great sucking edge. In those moments, love beyond earthly love flooded in. My wife became like Christ to me. Old hymn words, eternal sentences, well-worn promises began to tumble around in my mind; more came, then more, and then they became words in my mouth and I urged myself forward, forcing myself to claim what I thought was being denied me, slowly talking back, using your words, naming your Names, finding authority, and inching back toward your strength. And as this quiet, whispering Pentecost crept up on me, my wife and I continued to hug, even as Love from afar re-entered and I slowly knew you again; knew you to be there, to have been there all along, allowing these fearsome moments, and being my stronghold all along. Then, gracious Lord, a slow afterthought came, teaching me something even more about you.

If our hugging each other was another way of saying, "I love you," then hugging back and forth is a seamless utterance, two voices made one in a mutual and unstoppable song—call and response, response and call. So, Lord God, since it's true that I love you because you first loved me, then whenever I hug you—even in the darkest of nights—I have your word that you'll hug me back. Hugging back and forth—God and a battered soul. Hugging back and forth—God and a prodigal, homeward bound again and again. Hugging back and forth—God and a repenting church. Hugging back and forth—God and a cleansed child abuser, a healed alcoholic, a humbled narcissist. Hugging back and forth—God and whoever comes. Hugging and longing to be hugged back—God the Father, God the Son, God the Holy Spirit calling out to lostness itself; calling out to every person everywhere; softly, tenderly: "Come home; come home wearied ones, come home."

O dear God, O saving Christ, O convicting Spirit, don't relent. Keep hugging.

56

There is one body, and one Spirit, just as you were called in one hope of your calling; one Lord, one faith, one baptism, one God and Father of all, who is above all, and through all, and in you all.

—EPHESIANS 4:4–6

DEAR LORD OF THE Church:
How many times have you heard Christians talk about how they were "saved out of" Episcopalianism, Presbyterianism, Lutheranism, Catholicism, Methodism, Quakerism, "-ism" after "-ism"? But how does this fit with the fact that countless folks are saved and keep growing in the very same "-isms" out of which others claim to have been saved? Why do we dirty up all these parts of your body by saying we are saved out of them, as if they were the source of our sin, the source of our defiance of you? Why do we imply that there was nothing there to woo us to Christ, when at the very least (*least!*), we regularly heard your Word, confessed our faith in the Creeds and Confessions, sang truth-loaded songs, and came to your Table? And if we say that we have been saved "out of" this or that, and leave what we were saved "out of," won't we then find a faith-place out of which, sooner or later, somebody's going to say they've been saved? And if it's proper to talk about being saved out of a part of your church, then what about us evangelical conservatives, who seem to think that we're the safe harbor for everyone who's been saved out of something? How about the many of us who have been, or need to be, saved out of this safe harbor? I'm one of them, Lord; you know that. I, a preacher's kid, had all the faith-information a person could ever need and I did nothing with it, nothing, until that time when you broke into all the unused doctrine, the sleepy-time theology and scriptural ennui; until that time when you showed me that I was undone and empty; until it became clear that my conservatism was nothing without your personal Lordship.

Dear Lord, teach us this one very simple thing: No matter what denomination or "-ism" or faith culture we find ourselves in—no matter how much we hear and know about Jesus—we're in a no-Christ-at-all condition *until* we turn to him and him alone. Out of sin and sin alone are we saved; into Christ and Christ alone are we saved.

For that matter, Lord, once we've come to you, if more of us would stay around the places we blame for losing us—if we would stick around these places, telling out our salvation in no uncertain terms—maybe we'd have fewer "isms"; fewer migrating, nomadic church hunters; more frequent revivals, more local reformations, and a remarkably muscled and outspoken unity before the world.

Dear Savior, fill our mouths with Good News—positive Jesus-paid-it-all news. Empty us of negative, self-serving oh-how-I-sinned testimonies. Give us such shame for our sins, and such assurance about your erasure of them, that all we want to do is fill the world's ears with wonderful words of life. Let the beauty of Christ so shine in us, that everyone hearing us will know that what they *think* they need to be saved out of is no match for the cleansing welcome the Christ offers them.

57

For I was hungry and you gave Me food; I was thirsty and you gave Me drink; I was a stranger and you took Me in; I was naked and you clothed Me; I was sick and you visited Me; I was in prison and you came to Me . . . inasmuch as you did it to one of the least of these . . . you did it unto Me.
—MATTHEW 25:35, 36, 40B

DEAR HEAVENLY FATHER:
We have no one in heaven but you, and no one on earth but neighbors. Your Son made this ever so clear in the way he lived, preached, and loved. You were everything to him—his only God, his loving Father. And next to you, everyone on earth was everything to him—no exceptions, all neighbors. His unmatched love for you and his immeasurable love for us made the Gospel what it is, leaving no doubt about how his followers should live.

He made it very simple, really: love God, name his Son your Lord, go into every corner of his eternally beloved, vast world-neighborhood, and—without a thought of friend or enemy, rich or poor, privileged or outcast, young or old, sated or starving, parented or orphaned, sane or mad—tell his Good News, live his Good News, and spare nothing to see even one neighbor come to him.

Even though Christ made it all so simple, we want to muck it up— just like that person who came to him one day and asked for an easy-to-read definition of neighbor, certainly expecting to hear a pleasant, selective, localized directive that would fulfill the Law and gain him even more favor. Though we are prone to ignore it, this young man unwittingly spoke for all of us. Christ answered us all with one simple story about a running dog of a Samaritan, who bound the wounds of a running dog of a Jew; hostility befriending hostility, laying all malice aside and doing the work of redeemer and healer. For such is the kingdom of heaven. Without it we would be loveless. We would have no Savior, no hope, nothing but death.

Father, we all know this story (perhaps a bit too well), and for some of us, agreeing with it substitutes for living it out—for who among us would actually choose to cross the street and look the other way? Not now, Lord; there are too many incentives to neighborliness, too many whistle-blowers. Political correctness is here! How could we march against the grain of liberal fundamentalism? And civil rights! What incentive this! Who wants to be marked a racist? Equal rights! More help from fellow man, for who would want to be condescending "gender-wise?" And the threat of litigation! More incentive. Who wants to get sued for neglect? So, back to the righteous side of the street we go, back to the outcast, the wounded, the poor, the AIDS victims. Back to fulfilling all kinds of laws and protocols, helped along by all these new social incentives. Lord, it's not so hard after all. We're all of one mind, we of the new-founded global village.

Dear Jesus, so what? What have we accomplished? Of what is the kingdom of heaven? What pushes us to these newly-polished good works? Is it a matter of believers keeping up with unbelievers? Is it an attempt to restore the good name of the church and shut down outside critics? Is it connected more to an income tax deduction incentive than to redemptive love? Is it discovering new neighbors somewhere overseas or over the border and forgetting the family next door?

Help, please. Take us back to this one simple fact: There are no non-neighbors anywhere in this world, none whatsoever; pure love makes its redemptive and all-giving way toward anybody, anytime, anyplace, for Jesus' sake. Remove any selective mechanism from us, especially those that we've thrown holy water on; cause us to walk alongside the Savior, to whom every man, woman, and child is neighbor.

But Lord, maybe I'm just talking to you about myself and my own cradling of sin. After all, it was I who, just moments ago, mentioned all these outside incentives to neighborliness. It was I whose sarcasm tossed them your way, like throwing darts. I know myself better than I used to, and though I may have come a step or two in the direction of seeking new neighbors, I'm still in need of doing so with a newly purified heart—no reservations, no hidden criteria, no self-righteous back-patting my own "sacrificial" neighborliness. Turn me from blabbing brass and cymbal-clang, to the sweet serenades of love itself. Allow me the high privilege of Christ-likeness, of unmitigated love and unceasing surrender.

Then, Lord, if others see themselves reflected in this prayer, deal with them in the same merciful way that you deal with anyone who truly repents. And once we repent, keep us repentant. Keep near with the comfortable words from your very Son: "Come to me, all you who are weary and carrying a heavy load, and I'll give you rest. Now, go out into all the world and preach, feed, give, heal, share, bind up—no one excluded, everyone equally and freely loved. Go."

58

"... I will put my law in their minds, and write it on their hearts ..."

—JEREMIAH 31:33B

DEAR TEACHER:
Do we really need to mark up our Bibles? How can a red pencil emphasize something that's already its own emphasis? I realize that when I'm reading your word, something may strike and strike hard. It fairly shouts the truth, and I can't quite understand why it has not shouted before, so I mark it. But the simple truth that *all* of your word is Truth must mean that, sooner or later, our whole Bible will turn out red-pencilled. Then what do we do? Choose another color, or get another Bible and start all over?

I've discovered that if something—a verse or two—jumps out at me and feeds me newly, and I go for my pencil, when I look at it another day it will have dropped back into its normal place as a quieted truth among truths, not quite hitting me the same way. And then, I'll wonder why I underlined it, and I might worry that I've lost the sensitivity or the blessing that came my way before.

Father, what is a "key verse" anyhow? Is it something that stands out prominently, over and above the rest, or is it more like an ever-so-brief summation of an entire book, or the entire Book itself? If it is, then help us to go beyond rote memory, and take it in by finding a thousand different ways to say it, watching it multiply like loaves and fishes. Help us also to seek out more and more connections among all the parts of your Word, each part its own key to finding more and more keys: some subtle, hidden, and quietly at work; others loud, clear, ringing. Then your Word turns out to be both treasure chest and key all at once, everything pointing to Christ, the alpha and omega Key, in whom, and by whom, all treasures of wisdom and knowledge are stored up, unlocked, and ready for use.

Maybe, Lord, the only red pencil we should own is the Holy Spirit—the peripatetic Highlighter—at work according to his wisdom and knowledge of what we next need to know. As at Pentecost, when words upon words—tangles of them—became one single Word—known to all at once, Babel turned right-side up—make your eternal, written, living Word one grand, relentless, life-giving sentence. Help us to know that this sentence has but one Author and has neither beginning nor end. Give us the understanding and faith to walk into any part of it at any time, curious, hungry, thirsty, finding that there is no termination, finding ourselves always in the middle of something matchless: Truth itself; finding that Alpha and Omega is everywhere, completing every part as it does the whole. Help us to learn that there is no wisdom left to itself, no glory without a source, and no Savior from whom any single word can be separated.

Your Word is Truth. Thank you.

59

. . . There is that Leviathan which You have made to play there.

—Psalm 104:26B

DEAR CREATOR REDEEMER:
   I cannot get out of my mind the overwhelming magnificence of your creation: all that's going on—the shapes, colors, textures, creatures, explosions, implosions, speed, quiet, space, dark, light, timing, heat, cold, big-within-small-within-big, unimaginable coordination, unrepeatable events, age, youth, life, violent beauty, billions and billionths, no two things alike—so much to occupy you, to praise you as only stars and mollusks can; so much more for you to imagine, to start up from nothing or turn into something different. It would seem that what you've been doing all these eons in your vast workshop—what you continue to do, how you keep on imagining, how you change one thing into another, how you see to it that everything connects, how your laws continue the elegance, how you manage to keep everything running, how you even *know* a sparrow's fall or a photon's workload—are more than enough to strike any doubter square in the heart, and yet there's more and then even more.

   Yet, questions arise. I ask them politely. I ask them knowing that there are neat philosophical and theological answers to them, but knowing that having answers does not shut down the childlikeness with which I love to ask questions. No matter how infinitely Other you are, one way to get you near is to think of you next door, thinking like I do. So . . .

   What reason do you have for spending so much time, so much imagination, so much power on "useless" things—things in the trillions that are simply out there: luxuries, massive galactic baubles, one after the other, no apparent function other than to function? Doesn't all this display make you look somewhat overindulgent, compulsive even?

   I know that, in one way, you cannot surprise yourself. Nothing out there has come close to taxing you, or jumping ahead of your omniscience. So, if you know in advance what you are capable of doing, why do it at all? Is it partly because, like the child in all of us, you keep wanting to see how many things you can make with your magnificent Legos? Is there such a thing as showing off in a purely holy way to a heaven full of archangels? Does the Son say to the Father, "Let's try it this way for a while?" And does the Spirit say to the Son, "That's one way to do it, but watch what happens when I breathe a certain way?" Do you compete with each other in some spotless and hilarious way? Is this playing in its purest sense? Is this why we play?

Or, does being the Creator mean that creating is a necessity in order for you to maintain the title of Creator? Are you a creator because you create, or would you be a creator without lifting a finger? If it's not a necessity—and no decent theologian would say that it is—it must be an option. If it is, do you opt out of other things that stand up to your goodness, but you've no time for them? Or would you opt another way once the cosmos becomes, well, less interesting to you? How could an infinite being not lose interest in finite, infinitely lesser things (size is of no account here), somewhere along the way? After all, you had it all figured out before it sped off your fingertips, so why go to the trouble of making something you can already "see"? Is it that whatever you "see" cannot help but spring into being because you see it? Are your imagination and your Word, then, the same thing in two different guises: "I see and it is; my mind wanders and it is; I speak and it is"? Since both your speaking and your Word are spirit, is the creation, then, a way of seeing what happens outside of yourself when you speak? Is this creation nothing more and nothing less than a magnificent gift, not just to you but to itself—to us? Is being created a gift that cannot help but speak back in thanks and praise? And is it the thanks, the praise, the laudation, the declaring, the showing forth, the gift-praising-the-Giver that has the real significance for you? Can we then call this an anthem of love singing back and forth?

If so, dear God, I can see why you like to make things. If so, dear loving, gifting Creator, how lonely you must feel in face of our dumbness and numbness! Yes, the creation cannot but help praise you; the heavens have no trouble declaring your glory. In fact, they have stepped in more than once to do this—the rocks would earnestly and eagerly cry out in our place—and as much as the voice of your creation must please you, how much more ours might were it full-throated, pure, and unceasing.

I've gotten ahead of myself. Somewhere along the line, you decided to bring your actual Self, your spirit Self, to bear on the creation another way. You decided to create a race of beings made to act the way you do, to image forth every one of your attributes. Then and there, the cosmos—this vast, overly generous gift to itself—begins to make better sense, for is it not a magnificent prelude—not a tryout, but a foreseeing prelude—to something even more magnificent? With all of its mystery, beauty, variety, size, and sweep, is it nothing but a splendid artifact awaiting your company, expecting you to join up with it—not by becoming a mountain range or a pineapple, but by taking what you are, and what this cosmic bauble is, and making it into your image, Eden's crown?

Here we are then, Adam and Eve, the next-to-final ones, originally splendid, now dismally flawed, because unlike you, we chose to keep our seeing separate from our hearing. Lord, the most beautiful things make the worst garbage, and I say it again: here we are, pitifully fallen, blemished, corrupt, image-reversers, maximally opposed to you, lost without you, and fatally undone. And here you are, grieving, disappointed, rightly offended, even taken for the fool by the very ones for whom the best of your Kingship lay waiting.

So, Lord, this question still remains: Why do you even care about us? You tossed Lucifer out on his ear, and he is eternally banished. So, why not us? We've been nothing but trouble. We seem bent on inventing new ways to rip away at everything you are and have made. Nothing you do seems to matter that much, because what we choose to do matters more. To us, you are not so much God as you are a metaphor among idols—if that. If you were simply to chuck it all and journey out, out, away from us—away from killing and pollution and abuse, away from our self-crafted deities, our wars and sham victories, our coquettish devotion—no one would have any right to question you. And yet, even out there—way out among the galaxies; out where it would seem safe and quiet; out where you could distance yourself from dirt and skirmish and find a bit of Sabbath; out where you could continue your sheer, eternal man-child joy of making new things—even out there, just like right here, our stench leeches through. There is no Eden anywhere because of what we did to the one you made for us. You could even break out of time and space and rest in the eternities, but these, it seems offer no respite. And you could even break out of the eternities—they cannot hold you—and rest in your measureless infinity, and who could complain?

But no. A grand something as infinite as you takes over, and rides sovereign over the black and bleak—it's one of your Names. It's what, in the first place, presided over all the primordial seeing and speaking forth; it's what continues for as long as you do; it's what binds you to everything that despises you. And, above all, it's what explains your inability (May I say it that way?) to walk off, to find something better to do, to turn everything back into nothing and start over once more from scratch.

This name of yours is a working name. It's another way, a personal way, to say I AM and I ACT all at once. This name demands that you continue to stick with this crippled, contradicting cosmos. This name asks that, even now, you keep it working; this name, even now, surrounds your magnificent Son as he keeps saying "Yes!" to the atoms and "Yes!" to the grand laws and "Yes!" to the whole. Your mercy extends even to the heavens, and though we deserve the worst, you stay steady; you keep this magnificent work of yours running. Yes, I know; villages and babies disappear under mud and lava; winds straight from your storehouse turn trailer parks into whistling sabers; drought and flood choke and drown. But, Lord God, this name stays a worse fate; it intervenes and we continue.

And above all, this name is so powerful, so persistent, so overwhelming that you could do nothing less than give yourself—your only begotten Son, the first and final One. You went as far as infinity can go. You took all the seeing and speaking of your creatorhood and stretched it to its final conclusion. Seeing and speaking our redemption, you wrapped yourself in flesh and it was so. This name of yours became seeable and hearable. The Word became flesh and neighbored among us, joining the ravage and travail, the rot and rape of Eden gone sour. This name of yours, this seeing and speaking name is Love, Love Incarnate. This is the name that translates into the only Name whereby we are saved. It is the name that translates into the Alpha Omega name, your very own Christ, our Savior, this man Jesus, Son of God, Son of Man, God and image of God, the One who from the eternities sees our travail, speaks our salvation, and it is so.

For you do not just have a name, you ARE the Name.

So, Lord, I sum this wandering and wondering prayer up by saying that, yes, it is all of love. May I assume that every word and every fancy of this and every other prayer, from stars to sins to salvation, are lisping metaphors for this name of yours, Love itself? I think so.

I fervently pray that this name of yours, in the way I live, will become and remain the name upon which all of the Law and prophets depend. Please help me to love you, my neighbor, and myself the way you love, so that everything I see and speak and do will find no other name but Love to mark its way.

60

Is not this the carpenter's son? Is not His mother called Mary? And His brothers James, Joses, Simon, and Judas? And His sisters, are they not all with us? Where then did this Man get all these things?

—MATTHEW 13:55–56

Dear Lord of all Wisdom,
What if I imagined that your incarnate Son was born average? Would you take offense or would you agree? If the latter, wouldn't we have a better idea of what it means to be like most everyone else without trying to outdo them? And wouldn't we better understand what Christlikeness means?

It seems to me that if you had allowed your incarnate Son to be a genius, he would have had an edge over most of us, and we would have every right to think that we couldn't measure up. Our faith would be expected to ride unduly on intelligence. Furthermore, if Jesus had been a first century Copernicus, or a Bach, or an Einstein, then wouldn't we have read of some cultural upheaval, some grand civilizational leap in far away Palestine? And if there were no such leaps, then your Son's stewardship would have been more than suspect, wouldn't it?

Father, someone might say that Jesus' encounter with the temple doctors when he was only twelve years old, or some of his hair trigger answers to his critics, are evidence enough of an outstanding mind. But maybe not, and here's why: I believe that Jesus' averageness was directly harnessed to his steady study of the truth, to his growth in common wisdom, and to the authority with which he spoke and taught. According to Scripture, wisdom is something that can be prayed for and granted; it is something that comes of living dead center within the truth, making sure that Truth forges connections, draws out useful and widely applicable answers, and lives them out. Perhaps, Jesus came to show us how powerful an average mind can be when it is given over to wisdom—that it does not take a huge dose of brains to do God's word, that we are better off showing wisdom to the world than trying to outsmart it. Certainly Jesus studied as any son of the Law, any bar mitzvah, was required to do, but the beauty of your law lies in its utter simplicity, its basic comprehensibility, and thorough-going applicability. Anyone can learn it and live by it, not just barely, but profoundly. It's only when we try to outsmart it, as the Pharisees did, that we end up troubled, wayward, and lost in the inevitable tangle of ifs, ands, and buts. Studying to show one's self approved on your terms, with the beacon-sweep of your truth lighting every possible path, is a far cry from climbing the intelligentsia ladder. And for that matter, dear Lord, I've learned that loving ideas with unbounded curiosity—what we choose to call intellect— is Everyman's task, and not just for the super-smart.

And then, we come to authority. Jesus taught as one having authority, and perhaps people mistook the wonderful relationship between wisdom and authority for something "higher." "Where did this man get all his learning? Isn't he just the son of a carpenter?" But, Lord, isn't authority granted to anyone to whom wisdom, knowledge and purity are essential? How else can an ordinary person stand up and express something in a steadfast way, in the face of effrontery and scorn? How else can that person weather the outsmarting postures of worldly knowing, except through the calm strength that God-given authority grants? How else can humility and meekness find a home with strength, than through the authority that comes from you? How different and differentiating this is compared to power grabbing and power talking, especially the kind we so often use *on* people instead of on their *behalf*. And isn't it wisdom that tames power, turning it from over-lording to foot washing, and from "me-first" to "you-first?" Our dear Savior, a wonderfully average man, never confused power with authority. And when power came upon him, it was his Father whom he glorified, and his Godhood to which this power testified. And again, we must freely acknowledge that there is no relationship between power and superior intelligence. Ask of little children, out of whose mouths praise comes. Ask Baalam's ass.

So, Lord, where does this leave the geniuses, the mensas, the highly intelligent? Are they now excluded? Does this prayer bias itself against them, and are we to consider them freaks instead of gifts? Is all this talk about the gift of being average just another example of reverse snobbery? I think the answer is no, because what average people can do as dedicated stewards, the rest can do in the way you've created them to do it, because intelligence is not, and cannot be, the deciding issue. Wisdom is required of all people, and authority can be given to all. Maybe an Einstein can come up with $e = mc$ *squared* and I can't, but both of us are equally obligated and fully responsible to live out the common life-equations to the best of our ability, just as Jesus did.

Dear Lord, in these days of untamed over-estimation, when we cover up being average with grade inflation and prostituted superlatives, when we choose to forget that it is your decision to make most of us average, and everyone wants to win, and no one wants a "C" for fear of being left out—please re-dignify the commonplace and show us what it means to come *up* to the kind of average that you originated, that you equip and freely use. Show us that when Jesus became like one of us, when he emptied himself of his prerogatives, when he searched out and magnified his commonness by learning your ways, he showed us what everyone can do when surrendered to your ways, your wisdom, and your strength. Thank you.

61

And He said to me, "Son of man, can these bones live?"
So I answered, "O Lord God, You know."

—Ezekiel 37:3

Lord of repeated prayers,

You know that I am ashamed of how slowly I follow the simple commands in Psalms to praise you with singing, to shout your glory. Yes, I can make a decent go of singing, but I can't seem to connect it to praising the way so many folks seem to do. Nothing wells up from inside that I can actually call singing your praises. Nothing bursts. I can sing *about* praising by following the words that say "Praise Him!" but this no more means I'm praising you than reading a book of recipes means I'm cooking. You know that I long for a time when praise so conquers me that like David before the Ark, I will dance myself silly; like Paul and Silas in the slammer, I will sing myself hoarse. I ask that as I ponder this weakness and pray for some kind of breakthrough, you will grant me the peace that keeps me from fretting myself hollow and envying those from whom praise bubbles at the mere strike of a C major chord. I ask that you will burn away all the self-inflicted barriers that stop my lips and strangle my heart, and if I'm not built to bubble, help me to accept it. Either way, Lord, do your work, and cause me to know that you can at least take a measure of pleasure in the way I follow after you.

Yet Lord, what is a song anyway? What is a praise-full song? Need it be only its literal self—a string of pleasant notes and coaxing chords—or can you, do you yourself, take anything done in your name and for your glory, and transform it into a song? Does grunting my way through a day of ditch digging qualify? Does this become a song to you through the advocacy of the Lord Jesus? Yes, I think so, not because I have finally found an excuse, a stand-in, for singing praise, but because I'm striving to make a melody out of every desire for you, whatever I'm doing. I am comforted, because in your Word you have defined praise in so many ways that for hungry hearts and eager living sacrifices, only death can shut it down, and then only for that paper thin moment between the final earth-breath and eternal praise.

So, Lord, I'll keep looking without lusting for the time when I might be captured by song and liberated into the company of spontaneous praise. But meantime, I'll keep at this wondrous business of praising you with everything I do. And then, if a song bursts forth, even in the wee hours, I ask that it will not be some exceptional event, an unusual interruption, the ultimate achievement, a guess-what-happened-to-me event, but part of a continuation, just one other way to laud your name and worship your Son.

Amen.

62

But their eyes were restrained so that they did not know Him.

—LUKE 24:16

"Blessed are those who have not seen and yet have believed."

—JOHN 20:29B

ODEAR LORD,
 If you would just take skin to yourself, again—here in this time corner, right now; here in the yearning of my heart toward you, in the mix-up of quandary and promise and vagrant assurance; here in my house, welcoming chairs for you to choose; here, just an arm's reach away; I could ask, you could answer, we could discuss. Right here. Yes, right here, where "Why?" would be more than an echo of itself and "I love you" more than a Scripture reference.

And, yes, beyond the dusky gray of wonderment and puzzle, you would find that I *do* smile, I love, I trust, especially if I could connect your visit under my roof with those in yonder time—back then when you *really* walked and talked with people, went in and out of doors, lingered over the last crumbs of a widow's meal, replaced a customer's roof, and best of all, said, "Can I do anything else while I'm here?" This is how I imagine things. And skin would bring everything closer to home.

But then, what if you actually condescended once again? And what if you did make it a point to visit this piney spread in northern Idaho? This much I know: my dog would be the first to hear gravel-crunch, the first to the door; quickly seeing, knowing, remembering long-ago Eden-talk; keening a strange and warming song, savoring earth and purity together, ear-licking the one True Person.

But what would I do? "How," says the old hymn writer, "shall I greet you?" Would I recognize you? I've drawn too many pictures of you; I have so many impressions. My sketch book is crammed with starts and dabs and ever so few finishes. You're this way one day, and that way the next. How shall I greet you? Would I know it's you, or would I keep looking for another? For a better match? Are you the gardener, the chimney sweep, the census taker, the new neighbor? Which sketch should I trust? What have my senses come to expect of you, and has my heart so fixed itself on what to expect that were it not for this stirring animal beside me, I would simply ask your name and what can I do for you?

I'm not used to such quick knowing. Dogs are just dogs, aren't they? But dogs are faithful; dogs trust; dogs follow; dogs defend; dogs love. Dogs know. Cattle and oxen know; they've slept close by a Manger. Donkeys know. One once carried Mother and Baby down to Egypt, and another, the grownup Savior in a confused parade. Mountains, snowfall, rosebuds and heathered moors know. Rocks know too, and if the whole creation grew mute save one lowly pebble, praise unabashed would break forth, unafraid, unceasing, true.

I began this prayer by asking you to take skin again and now that you've come back—that is, now that I have slowly come to know that it may really be you, and, embarrassed over my slowness and sudden lisp, offering you a chair and we start talking—what next? How shall I hear? What do I say? Which one of the disciples do I impersonate first and next? And even if I go through the lot of them, showing how each has left an imprint; even if I were to tell you that if you had come just a bit earlier, my granddaughter's leg wouldn't have shrunk away; even if I've learned enough at church to behave properly in your presence, to repeat just the right things, this remains: How shall I greet you, strange Lamb of God? And how would you respond to my queries and frail promises?

I've known the answer long before this prayer began: You would have nothing new to say, but in the most patient way would take me once again through every written word about you, beginning with Moses, and I would know everything better.

But I still need to make this confession to you. I need to tell you that my faith is not yet near full strength; that the hope I have is not quite yet hope, because it tries to see. And while I have conjured up grand visions of the brilliance and cavorting joy that your visit would bring to my life, I also know something so dark that I'm afraid to confess it, but I will.

It's this: Had I lived back when you made your first visit, I'm so afraid that I would have been charmed, but not overtaken, by your birth; in the neighborhood after school, I would have wrestled you into the ground; later, when your real work was beginning, I may have tired of your stories, sweetest Savior, dearest Friend. I would have asked for more evidence; I would have nurtured the rumor that you were a bastard, and would have sided with your very own brothers and sisters. I would have wondered at your sweaty plainness and your irksome way of getting into my business. And given enough time, I would have followed you and that donkey in that perverse parade, and a few days later, cried out something that I dare not write down. O Christ! How can I bear your gaze!

O dear Jesus, hear me; hear me. Have mercy on my selfish imaginings and perverse longings. And thank you; thank you for coming to earth just that once, two thousand years ago, to plain-spoken homes and simple folks—you: swathed, suckled, strong-growing, meek and weeping. That thirty-three-year visit was enough; enough to take better care of me—us, everyone, the whole creation—today, than when we first believed; enough to allow a magnificent chronicle to be written—beginning at Moses, far-seeing, straining ahead; then fulfilled, preserved, and passed down through the ages—coming to us free of charge, bidding us who have no money to come, buy wine and milk and to eat; enough—more than enough—to teach the whole world the very same things that you would say were you simply to drop in down here, in your world just once more. *Gloria in excelsis Deo.*

63

Hope in God; for I shall yet praise Him.

—PSALM 42:5B

Lord,

If your thoughts to us are more than can be numbered—that's what the psalmist says—this must mean that we are on your mind far beyond those pitifully few times we acknowledge your intervention; your now-and-again stepping into things, even silly things like keeping the rain back on Sunday School picnic days. Lord, if your sheer power and sovereign control couple great and small events into purposeful partnership, and if it is true that all things work together for good to those who love you and are responding to your call, then wouldn't it make sense for us to thank you profusely by continuing to do every great and small thing alike for your glory, instead of seeking out separated praise times?

What pleases you most? Is it a life in which every breath, every act, every urgency, is freighted with worship and offered with praise? Or is it a life that sees praise a separate activity, an inventory of those few things that *we* think are most noteworthy, and then it's back to work, folks? It would seem that the first is preferable to the second. But then, what about the specific commands, the specific "inventory" in Scripture: to sing, dance, clap, rejoice, praise, recount and celebrate your works? Maybe the idea of a smooth, consistent, praiseworthy life is too general after all. Maybe the thought that, "Well, after all, my whole life is praise," is just a bit too intellectually sleek, a tad too brainy, and even emotionally escapist.

So, Lord, in that no one can be excused from praiseworthy living or praising while living, there must be something more glorious and rigorous and close at hand, leaving no one with an alibi. Therefore, please help all of us—your children—to strive for a seamless weave of the two: a praising, worshiping life, but within its flow and consistency, a readiness to break into alleluias and hosannas without reserve, without regard for time and place, without fear of consequence. Then, we might begin to understand even more what it means to be like our Savior. And we might also find a deeper connection between the infinity of your thoughts toward us, and the flow of our lives toward you.

Looking at it this way, Lord, we find these words from the same psalm grow into to their fullest meaning: "Let all those who seek you rejoice and be glad in you. Let such as love your salvation say continually, 'The Lord be magnified!'"

Please help.

64

Against You, You only, have I sinned . . .

—PSALM 51:4A

"I in them and You in Me; that they may be made perfect in one . . .

—JOHN 17:23A

DEAR LORD GOD,

It's very simple, once the right thought is given to it. It's this: I stand directly before you. Directly. Every second, every breath. Everybody does, for that matter.

There's an old gospel hymn: "Nothing Between My Soul and the Savior." And while most of its words don't quite get to what I'm trying to think through, the opening ones do. More importantly, there is ample Scripture to help me out, except I don't think I've paid enough attention to it down at its core.

Maybe I could start this way: What would it be like to get *behind* your Word, on eternity's side of it, so as to see you first of all, as it were, behind your Word yet one with it; to see your Word the way you, the Word, see it—free of language, uninterpreted? Could I stand with you? I know that if you revealed yourself completely, I would die. But I also know that you can empty yourself to any degree you wish, just as you did for Moses, without sacrificing one whit of your fullness. Even then, could I stand it? Could your Spirit usher me there, and would my Advocate help me live through the glory?

Or is this jumping the gun? Am I too encumbered with everything on this side—the time side of Scripture, a citizen of this gummed up and summed up world of circumstance—to ask for this, even with my paid-for sin and the sure promise of Christ-in-me? Am I limited to living on this front side of Scripture, having always to make my way *into* it, with your help and the guiding work of teachers and preachers? Is this the only way we have until the time when, seeing you face to face, there is no more Scripture, just you? Please understand. I am not demeaning your Word. It's everything I need; it *is* your Word, and I refuse to stay away from it; it is everything your counsel demands: your Son was its Living revelation, and he said that seeing him was the same as seeing you. But he, too, was emptied the same way your Word is. A Thomas or a Phillip or a Judas could look on him and live. And even then, facing the fullness of the Godhead, they still doubted; there was still something there on the front side of things that clouded and confused. It seems that just a few of your servants were taken into a different glory: Stephen, dying, crying out his sight of you; St. Paul, to the Third Heaven; Isaiah, in Uzziah's time; Moses, cradled in a rock's rift.

True. But unless you intervene far beyond my deserts, I must wait for that day when all symbols—including those that met their highest calling by wording out your Word—retreat into complete abeyance. I'm willing to wait. But I still think there's something more about standing directly before you than I've allowed myself to believe, even on this side of what Paul calls the darkened glass. I hope I can make this clear to myself as I continue to make way through this prayer. I know you know the answer, and I long to have it fully incarnate within me.

Your Word directly tells me that whatever I do, I do it *unto* you. I'm told that I live *unto* you, I die *unto* you. Even little Samuel ministered *unto* you way back when. Jesus said that whatever good we do in his name, we do it *unto* him. The psalmist says, "I will always keep the Lord before me."

But I don't live in a vacuum. My life is crammed with circumstance. There is no moment when there is none. I have a choice, though: circumstance can rule me or I can rule it. It's not so much that I can change a circumstance—that's not what I mean when I say I can rule it. What I mean is that I am given the strength to refuse its conditioning powers, its rule over me. If I give a cup of cold water, I can choose to believe that this act justifies me, or I can choose to give it by faith because I am already justified. If my house and lands are destroyed and I join Job, pocked and scabbed with disease, the choices remain exactly the same. It is only in this sense that circumstance has no power unless I succumb to it. When I do, I'm entering idol territory.

So, even though circumstance, by your grace, is ultimately power-less over me; even though a cup of cold water offered in your name is still a circumstance—a godly one only because it's in your name—and even though my life as a living sacrifice might include a mountain of godly circumstance, I'm still talking circumstances. And I know that *through* them, I can satisfy a portion of the truth that I live *unto* you. In other words, I live *unto* you both *through and within* the circumstance. This seems to be right so far, yet I'm coming to wonder if there is even more.

Maybe now I can return to the opening of this prayer, where I wondered what it would be like to get behind your Word on its eternity side, and see you first of all, uninterpreted. Maybe I've complicated things far more than I should, but what I'm longing for is to know you rightly, to live *unto* you, *apart* from circumstance, as if there were no such thing—nothing between my soul and the Savior. I want to live on the eternal, faith side of time and circumstance—confronting them, enjoying them, working and resting within their march. I do not want to see you through—or even in—the circumstance, but see the circumstance through you and in your direct and changeless presence. Or simply: "The just shall live by their faith." Yes, I think so, because faith is the life of not seeing. Faith *is* the substance—to which the seeable—the circumstance—is neither prior nor powerful, but subsequent and in submission.

There is one more thing. Sin—its exceeding sinfulness, into which I was born—is not a circumstance, but a condition that colors all circumstances. Prone as I am to sinning, when my sinning centralizes circumstance and it begins to wield its power, I must get to the other side—on your side of the Word—and face even the sin in my life as the wicked side of living *unto* you, so that I will not sin *against* you. Facing and defeating sin as *unto* you is the unique condition of being *in* Christ, whose completed work erases anything between you and me, the Father and me, and the Spirit and me. So, when a temptation comes and circumstance offers its inverted possibilities, I resist *in your presence as unto you,* on whom my every breath depends. It's you first. It's abiding in you, by faith, in hope, and driven by love. Thus, ever before I resist sinning, I am all the while living *unto* you, *within* you. This means that overcoming temptation is not so much overcoming the power of circumstance as it is continuing to live *unto* you. This may be another way of saying that living *for* Jesus is not enough, for it implies something like being on his side, or like casting a vote in his direction. Living *unto* Jesus is far different, just as being *for* him or being *about* him cannot be compared to being *in* him. It is *in* you I live and move and have my being.

Is this too much to ask? In these peregrinations, have I turned unadorned child faith into a sticky pastiche? Do I want to turn your paths into an endless maze? The paucity of my living and the strivings of my mind would say yes, but your promises say no and I choose to live among them.

65

Oh, the depth of the riches both of the wisdom and knowledge of God!
How unsearchable are His judgments and His ways past finding out!

—ROMANS 11:33

LORD, SOMETHING ELSE OCCURS to me about the numberless ways you think about us. Perhaps I should say the numberless *way* you think about us—no plural necessary. This has to be true, because you are both Beginning and End in eternal instancy. Successions of things, numbers of things, categories of things, sequences of things, are convenient for us but unnecessary for you. Everything is all at once, and yet everything counts one at a time. So, you don't actually count the hairs on our head one by one, for this takes time and implies sequence, and you need neither. For that matter, by the time you finished counting that way, we'd have lost a few and gained a few, and then back to recount. Sparrows neither fall, nor are they hatched, as if you were continually at the calculator, keeping track of the bird population. And if we put every particle of every known and yet-to-be-known thing on the table—every being, every law, every interaction, every act, every consequence—not just now (whatever now is to you) but always; if we took *our* sense of time, place, quantity, size, and distance, and superimposed them on your worksheet—of course we would get all riled up, lathering ourselves in doubt; panic even; wondering how you could possibly manage it all—especially me, right now, sleepless, 3:43 a.m. on a Monday.

No wonder our doubts multiply—we're used to things in succession and accumulation. When things stack up on us, we assume they stack up for you, except you have a radically upsized computer. And so we go, quantity obsessed, size slaves, sequence addicts, circumstance neurotics, fearful up-sizers, unable to figure out how you can keep track of all the nooks and crannies in your universe. And even though we have memorized all the biblical promises and best seller nostrums about your being "able," we seem incapable of "faithing" the chasm between finitude and infinity. We want to turn faith back into sight and sequence; we try to upsize you *into what we think infinity is.* And if we're really good at this, if we're pumping serotonin above capacity, we'll at least see you sufficiently bigger—"sufficient," more than barely in charge—and then we'll pass on our version of good cheer to those whose spiritual math is still wobbly. In any case, the half-filled and the half-empty believers are still caught up on one side or the other of the can-God-manage-it-all question. The half-filled folks say, "Somehow!" and the half-empty just say, "How?" All the while, all of us are creating you after our ways, idolators that we're prone to be.

Who can deliver us from these amplified versions of you? Who can take us beyond our ideas of magnitude and into the infinite truth of you, you alone? Dear God, it's true and ever so simple: faith can. It's your gift to us—that's what your Word says: Your gift of your making. It's not something small and human-sized that you shrink-wrap us in. No, dear Lord, there is a unique something about faith that is directly related to you and not us, to your infinite wisdom and might. This must have been what Corrie Ten Boom meant when she mulled over the difference between having great faith in God, and having faith in a great God. As with one truth after another, the burden shifts from us to you; to your Son's invitation to take his yoke and learn of him and trust how you manage. Then, when we ask you to increase our faith, we should really be asking you to reveal more of yourself, long before we would dare ask you to meet this or that temporal need. We should ask for faith *in* you as if there were none *but* you to look to. Instead of the kind of faith that we laboriously ramp up to match the size of the circumstance, we should ask for the faith that has no relationship to circumstance, but only to you; the kind of faith that is its own evidence, the kind that is confirmed by the sovereign character of God himself who rides the circumstances as effortlessly as he straddles the heavens.

This kind of faith is *in*—entirely *in*, not *about*—the God who thinks, acts, creates, redeems, comforts, controls, loves, and dies for us in his unique, all-at-once, once-for-all, numberless way. He is our all-in-all God: the only such One, the one Father of the only Savior, sending out the one and only Spirit, to tell us of the One in whom, by whom, and for whom are all things—numberless things—accounted for and brought to submission. Thus, St. Paul is freed to say, "In all these things, we are more than conquerors through him who loved us."

Thank You, Lord. Please, whatever it costs, deliver us from creating you in order to create faith. Transform false faith and increase true faith. Let temporal faith be born again and made true faith, newly and finally. Help us to keep our eyes fixed on you. Bring your way of working to bear on us and then urge us. Better yet, yoke us with your Son, to whom we look, whose burden is light, whose ways are sealed in the pure wisdom of the Father and forever secure in his numberless love and redeeming power.

66

Therefore they said to Him, What sign will You perform then, that we may see it and believe you? What work will You do?"

—JOHN 6:30

MIRACLES, LORD. WHAT A word! How we scurry about trying to find one! We use labels to raise the circumstantial to the dramatic, crassly calling this or that a "God thing." Thing! What circumstance is *not* a "God thing?" We love to stretch the slightest deviation from what we call "the usual" just so we can use this word "miracle." We glide into the superlative mode—turning exaggeration into laudation—just to bring you into where you already are. It's as if the ordinary is not holy enough, and if we can just get our spiritual pumps out and inflate the ordinary into the extraordinary, our faith is substantiated just that much more, and you begin looking good to the world, our comfort zones are expanded, and our witness is glowing. How artificial, how giddy, our blowing and strutting must seem to a struggling, beat up world, where fly-clumps nibble starving babies' eyes, where mothers and children are blown up by self-deluded terrorists, where famine is not a distant over-the-ocean-blue-word but an endless killing field. How unabashedly self-serving it is for us to think a raise in salary is on the same miracle-level as clearing those flies away, or raising the dead, or stopping the sun, or bringing rain to a continent of cracked earth and swollen bellies. There is such a thing as telling untruths about your work, creating signs and wonders that otherwise are humble steps in a quiet and stewardly journey. Have mercy.

Unless, of course, everything you do is a miracle. That's a possibility, dear Lord, a pleasant one at that, because it would keep us from straining at miracle gnats and swallowing everyday camels. The very thought of your taking any interest in us is miracle enough. For that matter, everything you do is supernatural—this is our word for what is simply natural and unceasing to you—and realizing this, maybe we should settle down into the sanctity of sweating and sabbathing *everything* through—naming it all worship, rejoicing in the way you are constantly at work seeing us through large and small, thick and thin. For this is where the glory is; this is where the Son of God, the Great Physician, the Good Shepherd makes his continuing rounds—quietly, unaffectedly, unceremoniously, thoroughly.

Dear Wine Maker, dear Multiplier of loaves and fishes, dear Death Killer and Foot Washer, teach us to calm down our giddiness and flowery one-liners. Help us to give radiant witness to the ordinary, *your* ordinary day-by-day path-finding. Lead us toward temperance, where the real mastery lies, where calm and consistent radiance mark our testimonies. Help us to understand that every ounce of your work is stupendous.

But, Dear Creator, even though all your work, great and small, is natural to you, there is still this straightforward word to contend with: Miracle. It's a real word with real content. It's a scriptural word. We have a right to pray for miracles. We stand in awe even thinking about them; we strain hard to see one and can't quite figure out why there are fewer than there used to be. We want you to do wonders with your creation. It's simple, Lord, when it comes right down to it. What we call miracle is what you would just call work—the kind of work where you simply rework your handiwork; where you ever so easily stop, start, reverse, accelerate, or change any particle of it; where you may choose to kill a cancer, or lengthen a limb, erase pain, start a stopped heart, bring rain to a thirsty land, or divert a grand national circumstance. None of these would add to your work load or tax you—you who can reverse every known thing in the twinkling of an eye. Your Son didn't work harder to raise Lazarus than he does at this very moment, keeping the creation in working order, or lighting up a grandma's eyes.

So, this must mean that our praying for miracles should take no more faith than our thanksgiving that the sun comes up every morning, or that Bernoulli's law is still in effect, because in everything, our faith is in you. O Lord, increase all of our faith then, every aspect of it. And give us the wisdom and discernment to pray for what we call miracles, not so we can brag about you and use the uncommon thrill of the supernatural to prove your existence, but so you will be glorified above all of our strident, subtle, sneaked-in gods and shallow god-talk. And also, Lord, please keep us from praying for a miracle just so we can continue to hang on to what we treasure. Keep us from looking for miracles the way your Son's contemporaries kept looking for signs. Keep us from building and testing our faith on the extraordinary alone. Keep us fire-bright in the daily walk and in the commonplace. Keep us from missing the things you consider significant while we strain to redefine significance to fit our rules.

But Lord, there is one thing more. Lord Jesus, help us to pray our heads off and witness our hearts out for the *real miracle, the continuingly possible miracle,* the truly supernatural work that you long for, and your Son died for: *the Spirit-to-spirit miracle of new birth.* Here's where supernatural work overtakes, recreates, inhabits, and enables our nature, finite and fallen as it is. Lord, look at our words for your work: salvation, redemption, conversion, regeneration, new creation, new hearts, new minds, new creatures, transformation. They all tell of a work that is completely out of the ordinary, alien to daily circumstance, contrary to human inclination. They tell of a kind of work that confuses, confutes, moves against the natural, cancels blindness, raises into newness of life, brings love and understanding to your Word, and brings new light to every possibility and every detail of existence. New birth: Now that's a miracle!

Dear Spirit, please see to the rearrangement of our prayer lives and our expectations. Help us to understand that praying for a relentless flood of conversions must take precedence over any other kind of interventional praying. God, put us to fervent praying. Lord Jesus, please do more of the redemption kind of miracle, even at the expense of doing any other kind. Dear Redeeming God, bring glory to yourself, vindicate all of your Names, and bring your Spirit to bear on the spirit of humankind. Please move on uncountable hearts and minds in this crushed and crushing world. Convict harshly and tenderly. Create all over again. Fill this blinded and toppling world with new creatures—not just a few here and there, but floods of them, everywhere. Break into the seemingly frozen hearts of terrorists, religionists, so-called hardened criminals, street gangs, prostitutes, pimps, abusers, tyrants, money grabbers, empire builders, and the uncounted millions of good-citizen sinners. And Lord, come back to the nations that have long ago slipped from light back into darkness. Revive them again. Let this miraculous work of yours shake the foundations of lostness, and bring the work of the evil one to a whimpering and sissified halt.

But, in any case, dear Lord, cause us to celebrate your infinite fullness, even when nothing looks right, acts right, or does right. If everything withers on the vine, and even if the procession of new converts slows down to a trickle (Forbid this! Withhold anything from us but this!), please keep us at work—celebrating the slightest breeze, the quietest sleep, the simplest glimmer of your love and eventual overcoming—knowing that your hand is just as firm and victorious. In Jesus' Name.

67

I have chosen the way of truth . . . I will run the course of Your commandments . . . . Make me walk in the path of Your commandments.

—PSALM 119:30A,32A,35A

DEAR LORD CHRIST,

It's clear enough. Your commandments are meant to direct us toward what we would not naturally do, and away from that which comes so easily to us. The commandments against sinning are hard to obey, but easy to understand. But when we get to the two greatest commandments, then the depths of our sinful nature are fully exposed, and the stark contrast between your character and ours is most clearly revealed. If love came naturally, there would be no such thing as a commandment to love. But we don't love, and in this we are most unlike you, even though you fashioned us to be like you. So, there it is: love God, love neighbor, even love yourself.

Commandments.

"How stern of you," my protesting self-righteousness says. "I've given away my goods to the poor; my body is ready for burning in its steely readiness to defend your truth. Nobody needs to tell me what love is. How can love be commanded? Isn't love supposed to be the easy flow from and toward another person that is natural to us?"

But there it is anyhow: "You shall love." In fact, Lord, everything noble, everything lovely and of good report, everything that brings us alongside Christ is commanded. Nothing is merely suggested: give, worship, trust, repent, sell all, prefer one another, sing, dance, sanctify yourselves . . . .

So Lord, help us to accede to your commandments, but, in your loving and gracious way, show us what lies beyond the commandments. Show us the new and fresh freedom that catapults us further and further into the very mind and love of Christ, bringing about a startling reversal. Now, because we so love him who so loves us, we *will to keep* his commandments.

68

Now I saw a new heaven and a new earth, for the first heaven
and the first earth had passed away . . . Then I, John, saw
the holy city . . . coming down out of heaven from God . . .

—REVELATION 21:1,2A

HERE'S WHAT I DON'T understand, Lord. Why is the creation turned
against us? Why are we pestered, harassed, put to death, by what we
call natural disasters and the insurance companies call "an act of God?"

I can understand holocausts better than hurricanes, because we in
our sinfulness are continually making up ways to take our neighbors
down. We make the choice. Nation overruns nation, religions persecute
other religions, gangs murder gangsters and innocent alike, the guilty
ravage the less guilty, and there is no good in us. We gather instruments
of power and oppression with which we subjugate, overpower, and an-
nihilate. We do these things because we want to, because we are first and
somebody else is second, because we thrive on the upper hand. We have
brought our lot upon ourselves, all by ourselves, and there is no health
in us. We pay the penalty of self worship by destroying our kind. Isn't
this enough, Lord?

So why do you double the penalty and throw Mother (Mother?)
nature at us, taking the lives of widows, orphans, the homeless—the very
people that are blessed in your sight, the very ones we are commanded to
rescue? Here's this inanimate conglomerate over which you have charge,
this creation of yours that we call your handiwork; here it is in its grandeur
and beauty, then suddenly, and with your permission, it turns ugly on us.
My theology won't allow me to say that you cause this, but only that you
allow it. But what's the difference, Almighty God, because, in either case,
everything is in your hands, everything lives, moves, and has its being
within you, and nothing moves a millimeter without your permission?

Dear Lord, I am afraid as I write. I'm upset; my faith shakes, and
my eyes don't see well into your providence and purpose, or, for that

matter, into your Word. I'm afraid because of my effrontery in raising these questions. I'm afraid that I'll turn away in disappointment and doubt, but I need to ask you these things, knowing that a family of psalm writers asked you similar questions. But there is one difference. When I go to the Psalms, the only complaints I read are about what people do to people in their sin, and how the consequences of turning from you lead to oppression and exile. Yes, I read of lightning and thunder and earthquake, but it seems more like showcasing. Watch this and marvel! It's kind of funny to think of Lebanon skipping like a calf, or the winds being drawn from your storehouse and the lightning stripping cedars bare while everyone shouts Glory! But what of those buried under tons of rubble? Or the tornados that come from your storehouse? And the floods? And their parched-earth siblings, drought and famine? This is not showcasing.

I know well about the nearly infinite reach of sin, such that the entire creation is in travail, in waiting. I realize that Lucifer's choice to overpower, and ours to reject you, put an entire history of reconciliation and saving work into motion. But again, Lord, why don't you stay creation's hand and, as cynical as it sounds, why don't you just let us go about the business of hurting each other without your adding cosmic insult to human injury? Why do things—*creation* things, but things nonetheless—destroy? In order that we can show our benevolence in disaster relief? In order that we self-destructive sinners can show a good, humanitarian side now and then? There has to be more; there must be.

Does it go like this? The creation, in solidarity, is mourning with our sin, and can only show this in its own writhing magnitude, its own tossing and turning and gasping. Is it this? Should we see these disasters more as Richter-scale lament and hurricane-force grief, the only way the creation can identify with us, the only way its own travail finds voice? Yes, I think so.

And could there be more? If our race is bent on oppression and power and hurt and ravage, is the creation doing more than lamenting and groaning? Is it trying to show its anger, to scold us, even in its own agony and travail? Is it protesting against the agreement we made with evil way back in Eden? Perhaps, the creation is also crying out to you: "Lord, why do we mountains and streams and animals suffer when we had nothing to do with Lucifer's lust and Adam's stupidity? Come quickly, Lord Jesus, take our pain and resentment away and save us all."

This helps even more.

But it still doesn't suffice, because I've not taken your lovely Personhood into account. You created, and continue to create the heavens and the earth in your eternal and ravishingly ecstatic love. And when we took this lovely creation of yours down with our shame, you went down with it and with us. And now, you dwell with us in all of our lostness; you indwell your handiwork (no, this is not pantheism), and as it groans and protests, you do the same. Somehow you grieve, and the ruach—your creating Spirit—groans with you, even as you give permission to the discomforting winds, the flexing tectonic plates, and a ravenous, sucking, low pressure area somewhere distant. What does it mean for your Spirit, sustaining and urging the creation from within, to be bruised and grieved, sighing and longing with it? How do you—Father, Son, Spirit—grieve, allow, sustain, and redeem, all at the same time, as an entire country, a wretchedly poor and oppressed one at that—Haiti, January 2010—is taken down, further down than ever before?

Dear God, help me. Help us. Deliver us from cute sayings: "Well, after all, sin is sin, and the wages of sin is death, and God shows His wrath by destroying the sinner and showing us how important it is for us to long for the new creation." Show us something more, Lord. First, increase our faith. Increase my faith. And then, take these cute sayings of ours and turn them around into powerful theology.

But please do more than that. Turn us, *every one of us*, around. Turn nations around; turn them to the Lord's Christ, the Son of God. Deliver us from evil, our self-created doings. Forbid that any believer, in these dark and destructive hours, turns away from you in anger or doubt. Instead, dear Lord, visit us with your own Spirit-driven winds and waves and shakings. Bring the late rains. Turn this world into a population of fervent believers, strong children of God. Turn the nations. Turn us all. Push us forward and outward in a rush of benevolence and Kingdom witness. Teach us how to fulfill your Son's commandment to go into all the world, preaching and healing, healing and preaching.

And then, dear Lord, when the next groan from this travailing earth finds its voice; when destruction swoops in, unwelcomed, frightening, killing, reminding; grant that heaven's gates will be overwhelmed, flooded, swept away even, with a host of those whose death is, in your eyes, exceedingly precious. Let the creation groan, but let the redeemed— uncounted in number—say "Into Thy hands…"

Amen.

69

Then a voice came from heaven . . . the people who stood by and heard it said that it had thundered. Others said, "An angel has spoken to Him."

—JOHN 12:28B–29

DEAR LORD OF DIVERSITY,
Why do I address you this way just now? Well, because I find it an amazing thing that we humans are so confoundedly diverse in how we think, work, and walk with you, and somehow you find a gracious way to teach and lead us into the grand possibilities of oneness in Christ.

How many kinds of minds and ways of thinking must you contend with? I know you made us, and made us variously, but that's not to say that we've sincerely developed what you gave us. There must be an invisible line, known only to you, between how you formed each one of us and how we have intervened with our own mechanisms for developing ourselves. And despite all of the nature-nurture talk, it's impossible to know, deep down, what would have come of us had we been born elsewhere, or had any earthly inventions taken different directions and perspectives. But here we are anyway, not necessarily frozen in our ways of thinking, feeling, and doing, but pretty close to it. So, I have some questions that, when you come right down to it, have profound meaning for the unity of the church.

Why are some people naturally narrow-minded and others broad-minded? Why do some people like to measure everything item by item? We nickname them bean counters, because that's pretty much the way they go about things. Why do others enjoy speculating or guessing, instead of counting? Why do some people think grammatically, and others poetically? Why are some more comfortable with the abstract, and others with the concrete? Why do some of us want everything spelled out, while others enjoy ambiguity? Why do some want to do step-by-step analysis, and others simply intuit or leap-frog to conclusions? Why are imagining and stylizing more like art, and measuring and conformity more like craft? Why are some people architects, and others engineers? Why do engineers begin with questions about why something does or doesn't work, and architects begin with questions of beauty and shape? As to the miracle of language, some want carefully chosen nouns and verbs simply to guarantee accuracy, while others search for the metaphorical, the analogical, and the adjectival ways of saying things.

And more to the point of this prayer, why is something as final and truthful as your Word handled so differently, by so many differently-minded people? You'd think that at the point where your Word confronts our humanity, your Spirit would guarantee that we would all commonly accede and commonly understand, explain, and proclaim it. You've seen to it that we have a book—Holy Scripture—in which specificity, variability, propositions, narrative, poetry, exactitude, and speculation are all comfortably at work with each other. We have the blunt clarity of Leviticus, the Ten Commandments, the dimensions of Temple and Tabernacle, for instance, but we also have the rich undulations of the Song of Songs, the Psalms, and the Prophets. And the lovely, in-between territories of the Gospels and Epistles articulate something of the whole, that only your Spirit can bring together and offer us.

It's true, there are the so-called black and white parts to your Word—and rightly so; but it seems that some of us only think in black and white, and demand *only* black and white from *all* of your Word, contented only with literalizing it. Then, there are others who love black and white, yes, but only as one part of a vast and richly colored spectrum of knowing and imagining Truth. More to the point, why have you/we allowed a certain word-for-word literalism to be equated more with conservatism, and thought-for-thought flexibility equated more with liberalism? Why are literalists so brittle? Why do they put so much trust in words—worshiping them even—that they fail to understand how your Word rises above words, bringing Spirit-filled luster to them, even as we try to freeze them into impersonal objectivity? Are they afraid of everything breaking, if one thing gives? It seems so. They find it so easy to say, "Well, if you want to think of thus and such as allegory instead of history, why then, the rest of the Bible is up for grabs and, possibly, so is your faith."

But there is a counter-question: Why do those who love shadings and variable meaning find it easy to take things too far their way, and allow undue "give" in your Word, relativizing nearly everything?

Why don't they understand that flexibility, left to itself, has no inherent strength, no fundamental holding power? Don't they understand that they are left with little else than a busied, circuitous backwash of ifs, ands, and buts?

Why, at the *extreme* edges of conservatism *and* liberalism, do we find a common, hard-edged brittleness at work—two opposing kinds of fundamentalism facing off in sniffy diatribes and theological counter-measures? Can't these double extremists understand that if something doesn't yield, it eventually crumbles of its own brittleness, or if it is made to yield too much, it turns to mush? Don't they understand that a structure (your Word, the grandest structure imaginable) remains whole and enduring because of the unique flexibility inspired into its fundamental inherency and truthfulness? It doesn't occur to them that a true believer could ever be any other way than "my way is Yahweh"; that there might be a transcending flexibility within which God's Word fully remains the only Word, the true and final Word, continually offering strange new Truth-doors begging to be opened—not only because of the temporal variegation in human language, lost manuscripts, and scribal fallibility, but because of the multiple ways God freely chooses to tell, and re-tell, the whole of Truth.

But I must realize this as well: While there are people on both sides that would give their lives defending the Bible as being the only sufficient written revelation from you to us, I am fully convinced that you, in your graciousness, have made your Word fully useful to each and every person; that by the wisdom of your hand, you will put up with their brittleness and mushy waffling, and guide them into more and more of your kind of truth.

Despite my questions, I can't forget that you just might be more than comfortable with all of us than we are with each other; that in some mysterious way, your Word works its wonders for the lot of us. The flexible and inflexible can commonly drink from the same Stream, and, instead of looking at each other red-faced, must face you—the Author of all Truth and all ways of telling the truth. And all of us must remember that our minds—no matter how they work—are flawed by sin, limited in their finite proportions, and, yes, pushed by the enemy, whose only design is to reverse everything, even to the point of relativizing the absolute, and absolutizing the relative.

Lord, unify us, not only by opening us up to more Truth, but by transforming our minds, no matter which side of the fence we're on. And then, continue to respond to the urgency of your Son's prayer that all might be one, even as you and he are one. Help us to recognize that *how* we understand is of less consequence than that we understand at all. Bring to all of our thinking the best of *all* ways of thinking. Lead us into a communion of thought-ways in such a gracious way that we not only tolerate each other, but move forward from wisdom to more wisdom under each other's cry for it. I ask this in the name of the One in whom both letter and spirit are fully understood.

70

Moab is my washpot; over Edom I will cast my shoe . . .

—Psalm 60:8

D EAR LORD,
The first verse of the Bible puts your Creatorhood ever so humbly: a universe at least ten billion lights years across, quietly, firmly disclosed in ten words—ten words that raise ten times ten questions and guesses.

What does this vastness mean? What is it like for you to see everything at once, full size? I know you're omnipresent, and I speak a little foolishly, but do you ever slow down and amble here and there through the distances, taking the measure of a black hole here, a quasar there, admiring a new-spun bolt of gassy gossamer at the edge of a faraway dawn and promising it a companion in an eon or two? Do you like explosions and gargantuan collisions, slam-bang-brutal surges of noise, fragments, and color? Is this somehow the little Boy in you, even as you once were? I wonder if your carpenter Son ever struck flint to tinder in Nazareth town, and remembered original fire? What about repairs? Interstellar triage? Do you fix things now and then—straightening an orbit here, bringing your quieting breath to an over-eager star there—all to bring a measure of comfort to the travail? Is a black hole an emergency, or a quieted fact?

Would you have designed time and light to slow down and fade out, even if we had not turned against you in Eden? Is it your nature to create and re-create, even if there were never a sin, a Fall, to prompt you? Or, do you look around, and reflecting on what old, fractured Paul of Tarsus said about cosmic travail[9], do you grieve every time something shows signs of quitting or breaking; do you wish that you could bump up the New Creation an eon or two?

---

9. Romans 8:22.

We know you are Mother, too—it's obvious—but who of us thinks of motherhood and cosmic explosions? Wouldn't a mother be more likely to give birth and nurture? So, what does so much violence mean to your Motherhood, unless it has something to do with the pain of birthing and raising wayward rascals? A mom would cherish, nurture, preserve, quiet, soothe, and tell sleep-stories to this rushing, ranting, ruckus. Do you? Is there something about you, about the cosmos, to which we are blind, because we think of you as the "Big Guy"—pitching comets like fast balls, or crashing through a star cluster without shoulder pads?

And then, why do you create with such variety? Is it because your imagination won't quit, or because you enjoy bringing gifts to the heavenly host and to humankind? Or, do you grow tired of us always complaining about manna, manna, more manna; so, from your vast pantries you shower us—patiently, generously, with endlessly varied sweets—more to keep us quiet than anything else?

Wouldn't you enjoy getting away from this battered, lusting planet; taking Sabbath in some remote quietness? Do you give provost-angels occasional charge of things, while you go off to plan another set of laws and natural forces, for yet another universe? Why is there light and dark, when you outshine them both? Why do you want so much space, when great and small are both the same to you? Why are these opposites not the same to us, since we are made in your image?

Here's another way to look at it: Have you created all of this size and variety to give us, your image-bearers, numberless things to ponder, to decipher, to use, to enjoy, and to turn into something else? This makes good sense; it shows something of what it means to be made in your image: You, the Creator, letting us in on your creation; teaching us to make things that lead out to newer things; teaching us to cherish the large, the small, the plentiful, the delicious; teaching us to take good care of it all. But how it must hurt you when we mistake this vastness for something to waste, something on which to sharpen our egos, something to worship—shelving you and adulating ourselves.

And Lord, I can't help but ask you a different kind of question about our conceited inquiries into the vastness. Do you continually change and shift the rules way out there, so as to keep the physicists guessing, scratching their heads, revising: gluon-this, superstring-that, dark matter somewhere, worm holes to other universes? Are you able to change your laws without our knowing it? Everything seems to work the same as always on *our* side of things, but on your side, do you keep ahead of the agnostic guessing game with new consistencies and strangely dimensioned realities? Perhaps, this is your way of trapping us in our own conceits and keeping us blind, lest we actually see; lest we actually credit you—YOU, I AM THAT I AM; lest we actually stop this godless primping and prancing and world-class guessing, and turn from our telescopes and symposia, surrender our equations, and whisper "My Lord and my God!"

Maybe this is what Jesus did, when he shifted the laws of communication from plain-to-see truth to hard-to-see parable; maybe this is what you've done to the God-displacers. You've kept the real secrets from those who think they're seeing into them. You've hidden them, making this vast cosmos more like a parable than a fact; keeping the blind blind lest they see, and keeping those who truly and faithfully see from the withering blindness from which they've been rescued. And if we see you first of all, if we own up to you instead of divorcing you from our discoveries—can the parable shed its skin and stand Truth-tall and plain to see? Is this how a humbled scientist can find Bread in the very heavens he measures? Is this why the grass is greener and the sky bluer to Christ-eyes? Does this mean that a humbled, Christ-seeking astrophysicist could actually do a kind of paradox-math, adding his big-bang equations to your Alpha-Omega Word, to come out with a throaty "Hallelujah" sum? I don't just think so, I know so, because this is what conversion does: It allows us to keep faith and sight in their rightful place. It allows us to live by the one, while celebrating the other.

Dear Lord, merciful Father, reverse blindness and false sight. Turn pride out and away and into the bleakness it deserves. Usher in meekness and humility, and then maybe we can inherit even beyond the earth. Keep us from making things add up to you, and if they don't because they can't, keep us from turning away from you, trying to make our earthly two-plus-twos add up to a spiritualized four. Help us to see you as the Infinite Sum, within whom all things cohere and make final sense. Turn us all to faith; turn us from the scattered thrills and privileges of knowledge and factual exactitude, to the One in whom all knowledge and wisdom are stored, ready to be shared; turn us to those who are led to say, "Sir, we would see Jesus.

71

Even to your old age, I am He . . . I have made and I will bear;
even I will carry . . . .

—Isaiah 46:4

Dear Father:

"How many olds are you?" This is what little kids sometimes say to grandmas and uncles. There's something about this way of putting it that goes beyond "How old are you, Grandpa?" "Old" is a kind of once-upon-a-time word that talks about the last-thing-up-till-now-right-now. But "olds" carries heavier freight. It's like saying, "Once upon many times," as if I could say back to my budding interviewer, "Well, I was once seven and then twelve and then thirty-four and sixty-two and everything in between and now I'm another old: seventy-eight. That's a lot of olds."

Lord, I know that I might be making more out of "olds" than little children intend, but maybe not. In any case, this way of putting the age question makes me think of you, not so much as the very old One—the Ancient of Days—but as the ageless, age-full One, the One with many "olds."

Here's what I like to think. When I talk about you this way, I don't just think of "olds" as age alone; I see age connected to the ways that a certain person, in a certain condition, at a certain time, *is.* If you are ageless in some curious spelling out of infinity—of no particular "age," and streaming timelessly within timelessness—could it be true that in your identity with us, you are every one of our ages, all at once, yet one age at a time *for and with* each of us, all at once—many "olds" and one "old" all the time? Without shedding one particle of your infinite attributes, while standing eternally needless and eternally complete all at once, while remaining fully God—Three in One in Three—couldn't you take on the diapered weakness of a suckling child? Can you actually become baby-like and babble "ab-ba-ab-ba-abba? (I'm not talking here about your Son's infancy, but about us all.)

What would it mean for you to menstruate for the first time; frightened, confused, alone? How does a teenaged Marine, caught in air-snapping crossfire, cry out—except to know that you can be not just spiritually there, but shrapnel-shattered as well? On the happier side, do you, now and then, simply have fun the way kids do, with jumping ropes and kites? Are there times when hop-scotching from the Milky Way to Andromeda makes up your Friday morning? Have you given birth— had a caesarian—alongside my daughter? And, more to this particular moment, are you a struggling prayer writer alongside of me, allowing some kind of bafflement or new idea into your all-knowingness? Mind, I'm not asking if you're actually writing these prayers—that would be self-canonizing presumption—but, are there times when you want to join me in prayer; to imagine what it would be like, *on my side of it*; to stumble into the glory of having an Intercessor, a Paraclete, to clear out the fog and tidy up the scrambled "whys"?

I ask again, can you be many "olds" for our sakes, without stepping away from your glory and blazing holiness? If St. Paul can talk about being all things to all men in order for the Gospel to be arrow-straight in its purity, I would think that you can be, too. I would think that beyond merely being with us—omnipresence pretty much assures that—you can be Baby, Child, Adolescent, Adult, Carpenter, Surgeon, Tentmaker, Composer, Plumber, Ditch-Digger, Nursing Home Resident, all at once, and uniquely each.

Maybe this is why your Son, as The-One-With-Us, turned his thirty-three years into such a graceful and natural walk. He became Everyone to every one. He did this perfectly, not to shame us, but to invite us into the fullness of our personal uniqueness, and to show us that all personal uniqueness is the same to him. Maybe, along with you, he had practiced being many "olds" from the eternities. Maybe this is partly why he, you, and your Spirit won't leave us alone; can't stop wanting everyone to find out what real carpenters, real marines, real lawyers, real moms can be, once they turn to the One who is already those things. And certainly, if he became sin for us, doesn't that say what I've been struggling to say, but on the deepest possible level?

What a Friend we have in Jesus!—this is it, isn't it? Does this make any sense? Will you tame any vagrancies in my thoughts, and purify the untoward longings behind these questions?

Please do. Amen.

72

For though I am absent in the flesh, yet I am with you in spirit . . .

—Colossians 2:5a

D EAR LORD OF A Thousand Generations,
The other day I sat down to read the Bible. In praying for
light and guidance, I asked you to be sure to enliven, once again, the
many words that I've read hundreds of times. I was afraid of a rush of
spiritualized speed reading—gliding this way and that; riding the sunny,
warming updrafts, forgetting the turbulence beneath; forgetting that I'll
have to land sometime soon, roughly perhaps, on disinterested earth. I
know, Lord, that there are times when you might want us to read this
way, because your joy—your personal, unquenchable joy—spills over,
and we rake in as much as we can of its abundance, in as short a time as
possible. And for those few moments we, like Peter, walk—or glide—we
don't really know—on Living Water, covering as much of it as we can,
tasting and seeing, tasting and knowing that you are good. Those are the
times when we are aware of being truly faith-full, swaddled in a lilting
calm; sure of that special flow of peace between the two of us, as if we
were enclosed in a kind of joy-parenthesis—no one or no thing around
to break into it—and there we are safe, sheltered, and cherished. I know
I'm mixed up in metaphors, but that's what happens when we can't find
the precise words, when your joy slips into our hearts and waltzes there,
and we join you, unaware of any downward pull or dark after-moment.

But there are other times when glide-reading is an affront, when
it comes of spiritual sloth and uncaring presumption. That's when we're
unconscious of anything between us except a wee drop of theological
super glue that promises eternal security, even as we dare its holding
power with our deadweight corpulence. In these times, dear Lord, when
everything is labored and heavily loaded; when there is no gliding, no
waltzing, no soaring; when the yoke your Son asks us to take to ourselves
won't fit, and the very thought of quick-footed discipleship is as distant

as east is from west; it would seem better not to read your Word at all than to grudge and trudge our way through the very words that once upon a time were honey and bread, light and life. Dear Christ, please show us how to urge ourselves toward, and into, your Word, no matter how our day is going, no matter how much we glide or trudge.

But Lord, I got sidetracked. I still need to talk about the other day when I asked you to enliven your Word. Not gliding or trudging, but simply walking through the normal paces of my daily readings, I wanted this normality to be alive and Christ-like, the way his everyday carpentering and praying and loving so vibrantly were when he visited us long ago.

This was my prayer, and here's how you answered it. You brought me into company with time's long spread, and into company with its many citizens: with trusting Abraham, and beleaguered Hosea, and street-smart Rahab, and love-wreathed John. I rode ground swells with Noah, and smelled a dank, salty winter's morning with Paul, ready to set sail. I found that incense really does have an aroma; and sweat, even on your Son's body, is a ripe reminder of work in a searing desert day. And locusts? Well, not so much in Egypt, as in John's lunch. Savory stew? Yes, and even Esau's lamentable foolishness—mine, too. Haven't we all sold our birthright, and like the universal prodigal, dipped in hog slop? You took me into the company of my often impetuous and lily-livered counterpart, Peter, and alongside him, my doubting twin, Thomas. And what does frankincense smell like? Well, very good, but no better than a smoky fish breakfast prepared by the Risen One.

But Lord, when you allowed me to join the ages of the kingdom, you also took me to the Pharisee's house, where I sat and ate with Jesus who, before long, had me worked into a snit, because I was one of them and not one with him. And later, I was at another Meal; I heard about Bread and Blood being mine, and I had to choose—and I failed. I don't want to go further, and you know why.

However, I saw Light sometime later and knew Truth in a stronger way; and come Pentecost, I stood tall with a transformed preacher (with whom I had warmed my hands at the fire on a shameful week-night) and "Amen-ed" with him—now infused with—drenched in—Spirit-courage and authority.

Lord, I want to live by Your Spirit, in the full round of your Word's stories, people and places. But enough can be enough, for here I am, having read some more of your Word on this particular home-spun morning; and now it's time to live in a way that continues your work, pressing on and away from, yet along with, all of your people. Thank you for history, but only as a fraction of *your* history and my next moments. And thank you for calling me—and a countless number of believing contemporaries—into living fellowship with you, and into the continuing work of history yet to come.

73

But one and the same Spirit works all these things . . .

—I Corinthians 12:11a

L ORD,
I'm thinking about when I'm alone and in that particular kind of quiet your peace offers, and your Spirit deepens, and I read: "Sing aloud, shout, clap, exult!" What then? Do I disturb the peace, or can I do these in spirit, continuing alone in the silence that you have provided, sanctified, and sealed? Is it possible that shouting can be spiritually rip-roaring loud and quiet-lipped, all at the same time? Is this an example of the Paraclete breaking into a rhapsody on my behalf, while I continue with the silence already sanctified by him? I think so; I hope so, because if not, then a disturbingly large part of my Scripture reading is hypocrisy and insubordination.

But then, there's the opposite: when we face words like these: "The Lord is in his holy temple; let all the earth keep silence before him." If we say or sing this commandment as a call to worship, what are we to do with praying, singing, preaching, and reading? Are we mocking the command? No, not if we come to know this kind of silence as shutting down worldly clamor and vain repetition. Then, the alleluias can break out, and the Word can echo and re-echo, as your kind of silence continues.

Father, I can see all of your Word this way—all commands as be-ready-at-any-time commands, as strong reminders that my life in Christ has no end to its variations. When Paul talks about praying without ceas-ing, he must mean something like this, rather than a continued litany that keeps us from doing anything else.

So, Lord allow me—no, please cause me—to live according to Jesus' words to worship you in spirit and in truth; in Paul's words, to be a liv-ing sacrifice; in the psalmist's, to worship you in the beauty of holiness. Then, my every breath, my every deed—whether heard or unheard, seen or unseen—is yours for translation into a consecrated blend of continued shout, continued silence, and above all, continued yearning after your very Self.

74

"I am He who lives, and was dead, and behold I am alive for evermore.
Amen. And I have the keys of Hades and of Death."

—Revelation 1:18

"My God, my God, why have you forsaken me?" These unfathomable words were inscribed long ago by a suffering, far-seeing psalmist; and then, dear Lord Jesus, you quoted them in the darkest and most anguished moment in all of eternity's expanse—"Eli, Eli," you said. You called for him, cried out to him, his back turned. You hung homeless, rejected on all sides; no place to rest, not even a manger-barn; no one to bear you up, no Father, love gone for an eternity. You reached back and drew from a psalm you may have learned from your mother; a psalm that tells a whole tale—one that begins with forsakenness and ends with hope. You certainly knew it in its wholeness: a dark-to-light tale, a resurrection tale, a victory tale. And there on the cross, had you the strength, you might have cried out the whole of it to your mother nearby, to the mob—for whose forgiveness you had prayed just moments earlier—and to all the lettered and learned killers who knew this psalm as well as you. They could have sing-songed it right back to you, nyaa, nyaa, nyaa, while you alone suffered its ultimate meaning.

During those terrible hours—and even before, in the blooded struggle in Gethsemane—did you remember the times you said "Abba, Father" over your thirty-three years of walking, talking, healing, and preaching? Did you strain to say it again on the cross, and it wouldn't—couldn't—come: Abba no longer there, the Father somehow forsaking even himself in forsaking you; the Spirit unable to come down on you, no longer your Dove-Comforter, your Paraclete, your *ruach*; the Godhead silenced and absent except for your isolated cry. You—very God of very God—were separated eternally from your own fullness—the fullness of your Father depleted in your depletion; the Godhead infinitely curving away from Itself; you, emptied beyond your self-emptying, there on the cross, but not there; God forsaking God, eternally absent in the per-plexing mystery of his Triune presence—weakened beyond measure, yet omnipotently atoning once for all.

How can I say? Who can ever say? Yet, who can hold peace?

Dear Savior, how many times in your daily walk did you go over this psalm devotionally, as I often have, savoring the final glory, mulling over the strong victory-words that pelted and overwhelmed the taunt-ing ones? Were there times when even you might have skipped over the opening cry, because the outcome was so clear to you? Or did that psalm come hard at you, time after time, striking you blunt-square, meant only for you, buckling your knees? Did Satan himself wreath it with such filth and off-scouring that more than once you turned away, Gethsemane already on your horizon, the cross dress-rehearsing itself again and again, forsakenness jabbing as you lay down to sleep and again as you awoke to a morning sun gone gray? Is this why you went off alone to a mountain? To find Abba there, to seek solace, to hear him once again say how pleased he was with you, to find rest in his everlasting arms, to talk openly with the same Spirit that on a distant Friday would not speak up for you?

Dear Jesus, my Lord Jesus, God's very Christ, only Savior, I can't step over to your side, the Cross side, of my sin. My side, the way I see it—even with your Spirit's help—is ugly enough; but I don't see it vividly enough, because sin blinds sin. I can only guess at its full weight; the rest I must leave to you, trusting you to understand that even my tears of repentance—those few I've shed—are tainted by the very sin I confess. You alone know this; you alone know how to bear with sin-weakened confession; you alone can cleanse it and make it into a fully honest plea, a pleasant aroma, pure and unsullied; you alone can fill it to the full with your righteousness, even as you were once made into the very sin that keeps taking me down, sin by sin.

Dear Jesus, something else strikes me about that fragmented Cross-cry. There's a two-letter word without which yours would be a normal, earth-bound, despairing question. But with this word, your cry became the greatest prayer of faith ever uttered. In total abandonment—your body torn by its own weight, your whole person—God and man to-gether—blackened and bearing the full weight of the world's sin, your perfection somehow surrendered and turned into sin itself—then and there, you claimed your absent Father to be yours, *still*. You said "My—

My own, *My very own*—God." May I assume that somewhere hidden in "Eli, Eli," was that child-cry: "Abba, Abba, Father, Daddy"; still there, still unquenchable? And in that eternally extended moment—when utmost Evil held you captive—your prayer, your faith-drenched owner-ship of Eli-Abba, was the uttered assurance that Evil would be put to flight, overcome forever by your Blood, even while you were entering into forever's punishment.

O Christ! Save us from the twin blasphemies that trample and de-mean the full weight of possessing you in utter forsakenness. Save us from the flood of "ohmygods" that we spew, vomit, giggle out, and croon at the drop of the flimsiest happenstance. Save us from that circum-stantial, self-pitying, self-worshiping exaggeration, "Yesterday I went through hell," or, "It was a hell of a week." This said, Lord, I know that the world's holocausts bring us close to these words: I know that a despair-ing mother wonders how much worse it can get, while she watches her three-year-old turn yellow-bald from chemotherapy; I know that, right now, hundreds of thousands of your children are trapped in mud, debris, disease, corruption, unnamable abuse, and homelessness—earthquaked, tornadoed, car-bombed, famined, droughted, deserted, and manhandled beyond belief. I know this, and I pray that I will share their burdens, through your direct guidance, for as long as I have breath.

Dear suffering, weeping, angered, redeeming God—keep our hearts humbled and our lips under your control. And if, in our struggle to enter into Christ's sufferings and desolation, we have occasion to wonder if and why you may have forsaken us, grant us the same faith that your Son had, and help us always to possess you, even as he did. Help us by your Spirit always to say, "MY God, my personal, my very own God." Then, give us the very same completeness to this prayer that the psalmist penned, and your Son knew so well. Help us always to read the end of the story and not just its dark beginnings. In Jesus' Name.

75

"You have heard that it was said, 'You shall love your neighbor and hate your enemy.' But I say to you, love your enemies, bless those who curse you, do good to those who hate you, and pray for those who spitefully use you and persecute you."

—MATTHEW 5:43–44

Lord,
I can't think of any other way to put this except to say thank you for allowing some really sour-headed praying to be included in your Word, right along with the sweetest utterances known to humankind. Sometimes, in the same prayers even, we come headlong into sour and sweet knocking heads together. It's unsettling, and no more so when an unbeliever asks how a loving God would ever allow this kind of talk in his Word.

"Here's your god," they say, "asking us to pray for our enemies, but turn back a few hundred pages and there's an angered psalmist dripping blessing-words on those who take his enemies' children and break their heads against the rocks. And what about the countless times the psalmist asks his god to destroy everyone who threatens and works evil against him?"

What do I say? Do I join the hair-trigger cynics who call this just another example of the inconsistencies and contradictions sprinkled throughout the Bible? Do I then undertake my own kind of editing and choose only what I believe to be your Word? Do I find some mealy headed rationalization, or a dispensationalist smooth-over to steer your Word away from any semblance of mistakenness? No, I won't do that, not any more. Nor will I give up on the conviction—stronger than it's ever been—that Scripture, from start to finish, is your revealed Word, every word of it.

Here's what I'll do, though; I'll say this to the skeptics and the perfectionists: "God, Almighty God, is so sure of himself, so overwhelm-

184

ingly true to his truth, so openly frank about the presence of sin in the hearts of even his most ardent followers, that he—through his Spirit—will allow sinful praying to show up in the Bible's primary prayer book, in order to show us the *wrong* way to pray when things go against us. He cannot hide sin; he'll never make excuses for us. He knows how to tell the truth without compromise. He is honest about us, and about how he speaks about us. He is eternally assured of his ways and knows that they override weakness and folly, even among his disciples."

And I'd continue: "He allowed the story of Paul and Barnabas' spat and parting of ways to be included in the chronicles of the early church, without letting us in on who was right and who was wrong. He allowed Peter's recurrent cowardice amongst the judaizers to be reported—Paul faced Peter down and called him, along with Barnabas, a hypocrite. God was not at all afraid to show us this side of Peter—even as God sent his Spirit upon him to pen two of the sweetest epistles in the New Testament. God openly showed faithful Abraham's faithless duplicity about Sarah being his sister instead of his wife. God told Hosea to marry a prostitute-adulteress in order to symbolize Israel's spiritual whoredom. In his Son's earthly genealogy, he did not hide the facts about tawdry Judah, from whose tribe Jesus was descended. He is not afraid, this truthful God of ours. And this is why his Word remains truthful and utterly trustworthy. We can read it and find ourselves, time after time—walking alongside a murderous adulterer, a man after God's own heart; keeping step with the flawed apostles, smack in the middle of triumph and trouble; praying wrongly as the psalmist did; praying at cross-purposes and being included in the ranks of the faithful; living contradictorily, worshiping idolatrously, and being kept whole while being warned, even chastised. In all of this, it's the truthfulness of God that comes away shining bright and clear—even when, in St. Paul's words, it is preached in envy."

That's what I'd say. Thank you, Lord, for the way your perfect freedom walks hand in hand with your spotless holiness. Thank you for being Truth itself, for always telling the truth, and for the way your fearless honesty leads us directly to your only Son, in whom all treasures of truthfulness are made ours through his saving power.

So, dependable Father, I join the writer of Psalm 119—all 176 verses—and Psalm 19 in making this confession: I love your testimonies, knowing that your word is a lamp to my feet and a light to my pathway, sweeter to my mouth than honey, and more to be treasured than the finest gold. As I study your truth, I will praise you yet more; I will keep your testimonies forever and ever; I will speak of them before those who taunt me, even before kings; and I will not be afraid nor put to shame. And pledging myself this way, I tell you also that you have been good to me, even as you have afflicted me and taken me down, so that I might be raised up to learn even more about your testimonies. You are good, O Lord, and what you do is good. Thank you.

76

And in Your book they all were written, the days fashioned for me, when as yet there were none of them. Such knowledge is too wonderful for me; it is high, I cannot attain it.

—PSALM 139:16B, 6

THERE IS SOMETHING ABOUT your grace and mercy that I don't think of often enough, and it's connected to your omniscience. Both you and I know that sin is always with me, and no matter how hard I strive to keep growing toward the height of my Savior's stature, I stumble and stumble again. Your mercy and comforting forgiveness are at work in the face of this. Far more than merely keeping up with these sins, you outrun them and remove them from me, as far as east is from west.

But here is something amazing enough to bring joy and caution into a waltzing oneness. You know what I'm going to do tomorrow, and the next day and the next, and I don't. But both of us know one thing for certain: It won't be all roses; I'll sin, not by plan but by nature. The amazing thing is that while you know this right now—while you know that somewhere in my future, I, like David, could sin grievously; or, like Peter, deny you, having just told you I'd follow you anywhere—while you know things like this about me, you, *at this moment*, bless me as if a shameful tomorrow won't happen. In turn, rejoicing in your generosity, *at this moment*, I celebrate your morning-by-morning mercies, confess where I've gone wrong, and strive to grow in my walk with you; never planning that one day far off, I might turn from you. But here you are with me *now*—urging me, nurturing me, teaching me, blessing me—as if nothing dark and horrible were to mark a future moment.

I realize that there are nicely packaged theological explanations for this; that Jesus died for all my sins—past, present, and future; that Christ's sacrifice was a once-for-all work, against which neither time nor circumstance has any force, whatsoever. I realize that, according to some of the packaging, there is both comfort and danger in saying that I am eternally held, that no one can pluck me out of your Son's hand. And, to blur things more than a little, I also know that other theological packages make things a little more precarious, warning me that I can actually lose my salvation and then start over again, born again and again and . . . if I choose.

Lord, theological packages are just that: packages—containing only so much boxed-in, boundaried speculation; wrapped neatly, tied with an identifying ribbon, put alongside other packages tied with their own particularized ribbons, and delivered to pre-selected theological zip codes. But they're unsafe, left to themselves, for what they don't seem able to do is put *all* of your Word together—free of dimensional limits, and opened to the complete, eternal, mysterious, infinite, intertwined, and freely resonating harmony in your Triune mind. You know that I'll sin, yet you bless. I know that I'll sin as a matter of nature, yet I must flee from it, breathless, and should never assume that I'll do anything but avoid and hate it, and, as the book of Hebrews says, even strive against it to the shedding of blood.

So, Lord, I can neither rest in the promise of grace *all by itself*, as an abstraction, an automatic given; nor can I live in fear of falling flat and worrying that your grace will be proportionately cut back or run low. Similarly, I pray that I'll be kept from measuring the mercy shown me today by your knowledge of what I'll do tomorrow, lest I fall into the trap of measuring today's grace by what I did yesterday: living on tomorrow's or yesterday's works, instead of continuing faith. I pray that in and of themselves, joy, godly fear, reverence, and perseverance will mark my sojourn. When I fail you, I pray that my repentance will be immediate, almost irrespective of grace—simply because I have failed *you*, sinned in your face, hurt you—and I want to say I'm sorry knowing that I do not deserve grace.

Lord, how comforting to know that the acceptable time is always now; that you somehow empty yourself of omniscience on my behalf and work with, for, and on me *now*; laying your all-knowingness aside in your watch over me, your outpouring toward me, and my walk with you. So, I pray that now and now and now and now will be the incessant, unceasing moment within which I live, just as your grace, always all-sufficient, is now here, always now here, always . . . always. Amen.

What does it profit . . . if someone says he has faith but does not have works? Can faith save him? But someone will say, "You have faith, and I have works." Show me your faith without your works and I will show you my faith by my works.

—JAMES 2:14, 18

D EAR ALL-WISE GOD,
I came onto something recently that helps me better understand why biblical interpretation and theological positions can be so much at variance within themselves and with each other. I got to thinking about the way light and matter appear to behave like waves in one context, and particles in another. And I made a connection.

Before going on, I attest that your truth is fully Truth—from the tiniest jot clean through the entire whole. There is no break in its consistency. All of it coheres in you, the Living Truth, and there is simply no way it can deny itself, shift its direction, confound itself, or make excuses, anywhere throughout its length and breadth.

So, when I think of waves and particles, I'm reminded of your Word, both in its blunt force and dove-soft welcomes. I reflect on our seeming inability to think uniformly about *its* uniformity. Is there something in your Word, in its all-encompassing richness, that feeds us and eludes us at the same time? Does your truth "behave" in somewhat the same manner as matter does, showing itself one way ("wave-like?") in one place, and then another way ("particle-like?") in a different place, *without once changing its nature*? Is your truth so multi-faceted that as your Spirit directs and as language allows, it shines a certain way on one passage and another way in another passage? Is your truth like everything else about you—so inexhaustible that it simply can't be pinned down to fit into one or two, or a hundred verities, or be fully explained in any one place or instance? Is your truth such that all of it is needed to explain all of it?

Dear Lord, there are other kinds of richness that make the study of your word even more challenging. Your Word must make use of human words. The same verb or noun in one context shows a different face than in another and another, and then another. Next come the adjectives, the adverbs, the metaphors—the nuancing, tinting devices that grace our expressions, offer a thousand shifts, whet our imaginations, and widen our vistas. Here they come, these curious word-trains, populating your Word. Next follow the interpreters, the commentators, and the summarizers, each with a slant on your ideas. And when we multiply the uniqueness of one language by that of a thousand others; by the cultures of countless times and places; by the sweep of time itself; by stylistic differences from author to author; by the semantic differences among poetry, prose, and proposition; by the mysteries of the Triune Godhead; by the fallibilities and biases of the interpreters; we find ourselves in a kind of Truth-woven, Truth-seeking labyrinth.

So dear Lord, it's not just one or two kinds of richness to your Word, is it? Our ways are so limited, and your ways are ever so finely wrought—far beyond the finitude of words, even as they swaddle your Word. Your truth is Truth, yes, but we're faced with seemingly numberless angles from which to view the same changeless verities. And when we limit ourselves just to certain angles that seem to act the same way, and overlook or ignore the ones that seem to act another way, we end up short-focused, even though we may have written volumes to articulate our "understanding." So, maybe this is why, for instance, John Calvin saw everything wave-like and John Wesley saw everything particle-like. Maybe this is why there is disagreement about when sanctification starts, or where our Lord is to be found when Bread and Wine are lifted up. Lord, you know, there's more even than this.

I keep on thinking, wondering what's on your mind as you look down from the top—clasping every single heart of the sojourning, opinionated pilgrims in the labyrinth: pilgrims certainly never lost, sometimes confused, often biased, yet resting and working, praising and wondering. Maybe you're saying something like this:

"I know there's difficulty down there. But had I wanted my Truth squeezed down into a one-dose, cure-all, clone-all, and my children to be one-dose, one-way robots; I could have done that and spared the church a lot of trouble. But I decided to let my Word soar in infinite air, even as it condescends to live and take its chances on earth; yes, within these curious

things called words. I could have frozen all of them solid, so that each single one, for all time, would have an obediently singled-out meaning and would combine into little gear trains, dutifully driving my lock-stepping robots down generic pathways—and that would be that. And the straight and narrow would be no more than a conveyor belt.

But that's not my way. Within the flawed and finite minds of scholars, theologians, and interpreters, my infinite Word continues to lodge, germinate, probe, work itself this way; it finds and attaches a certain nuance here, another there, and still more in my revealed counsel and written Word. My control of Truth—I am its Author and Finisher, don't forget—is such that I not only transcend all these earthbound vagaries and foreshortened doctrines, crafted by those who would die defending my Word, but I turn them to my advantage, to my glory—time after time, place after place."

And then, perhaps, I hear you adding this:

"But why do my children latch onto single nuances, as if they were the only ones? Why do they isolate them one from another so that, in contrast to the way I provide a treasure trove of possibilities, they can only see waves or only particles, when I see everything all together and all at once? Why do they take identical facets and build their edifices out of them, only to discover that someone else has isolated their collection of identical facets and built their counter-edifices? Don't they understand that despite their love for my Word, they could be taken further into the Truth-distances of which I'm the Master? Why do they stop and pitch their tents, homesteading on paltry acreage when they could keep going, even if, like Abraham, they don't quite know where? Why won't they face first things first—the paradoxes and the mysteries, the chief cornerstones—as their beginnings? Instead they treat them after the fact, finally admitting to "the mystery and wonder of it all." Why do they own up to mystery only after reason and systems have run their course?

Perhaps, you would conclude this way:

"But I am patient. The Church will be built, even when the world can't figure out which church is the Church. I am patient, now as I have been, with my chosen people from way back when; people relentless in their shortsightedness and stubbornness, persistent in reading my Word their way and applying it their way, ears too soon closed. I sent my Son, the Living Word, and even he had trouble making his clarity clear and his wisdom wise. And as I have watched the greatest thinkers and the most mundane ones, each a little too biased for my liking, I will not leave them

alone. I will not turn away. I will persist. My truth, in all of its wondrous reach, is still working, and will do so until faith is turned to sight; and all the company of labyrinthians will know even as they have been known all along."

Dear persistent Master, bear with these imaginations and help me to do better with your Word than I've ever done before. Open my eyes so that I won't sleep the sleep of the partially informed and narrowly convinced. Help us all—scholars, evangelists, preachers, teachers, laypeople—to reach further up, down, and in. Help us to find new ways to say your truth in our own words, to the end that your Word to us and our words back to you are opulent and harmoniously interwoven, as never before—neither narrowly locked up nor prodigally relativized. Thank you for all the theologians, the scholars and the exegetes, for they love you and tower above a major part of the rest of us. Honor them by enriching them, enlarging their borders, harmonizing their passion, and leading them like a Shepherd. Honor yourself by bringing unprecedented wisdom to them; raise up countless messengers to follow, generation after generation, who will bring delight to you looking in from the top, and will bring searing insights and persuasive evangel to those who live in your world.

In Jesus' Name.

78

And while they looked steadfastly toward heaven as He was taken up,
behold, two men stood by them in white apparel, who also said,
"Men of Galilee, why do you stand gazing up into heaven?
This same Jesus . . . will so come in like manner . . . "

—ACTS 1: 10–11

DEAR LORD,

If we were to put to print all the pictures—the billions upon billions of them—that our believing minds have made of you down through the ages, what would we have? Not much really, except momentarily thrilling, confounded, blurry, fleeting, unstable, transient, vision-thoughts that fail to suffice fully; vision-thoughts that flirt with the edges of idolatry, then slip away for another time; vision-thoughts whose only cleansing is immediate blindness, whose only hope is faith-in-waiting and the Word made flesh.

Dear Father, you know how hard we struggle this way. You know that loving you with all our might, we want to come upon that shining finality, the infinitely rendered, glory-washed One whom we can see with the same clarity and assurance that burly maple and snowflake and sunshine afford. "Show me your glory"—here and always we join Moses' cry, but we seem never to see what he saw, unless a certain glory passed us by while we were looking at our own picture book. And if you were to come to us in unmistaken, unplanned brightness, would we know what to do, except blubber? Or, rescued from a running tongue or an urge to find a guitar somewhere, and struck instead with dumbfounded silence, would we lock that moment up for good, for ready reference in time of need? And would we then have another idol—given substance by the ploys of memory—praying to it instead of you, expecting a repeated glory, a similarity, a duplicate assurance? And would you then, in your mercy, crush the memory and urge us ahead into fading light, as you did veiled Moses, pleading with us to forget in order to keep seeing? I pray so.

Dear God, how we treasure treasure; how, like the unfaithful steward, we bury it, afraid to cast it forward into newness; how, like old Scrooge, we get out our spiritual cash box now and then—fondle it, clutch it tight, count it once more, hide it once more. And when your patience overcomes our mistakenness, and you reach down into us and reveal yourself in a new way—with a still, small voice—please keep us from missing it because it doesn't seem to match what we already treasure. Keep us from asking, like Phillip, for a vision of you, even as your Son stares us smack in the face.

Unless, Lord, unless you see deep into and behind these sincere, queer idolatries; unless you see through the falleness that stains our walk and compromises our hunger. Unless you understand that in soul-depth, all true seekers share a loving, persistent, pure yearning that tries, longs, tries and longs after you with a thirst whose primitive consecration and ardor are themselves pleasing to you, sufficient for you. Lord, how we need to remember that you make your home in the depths of our longing, eternally before and after any image of you appears. How we need to remember that your desire is for us to see you *within* our longing, not somewhere outside of it. And as you sanctify this longing simply by continuing to intensify and inhabit it, keep us from looking for another golden calf, another concretion, another fleeting fantasy. Instead, lead us out and away, out and away. Drive us toward Abraham's wagon tracks, Habbakuk's famine pledge, the widow's robe touch, Paul's and Silas' night song. Open our eyes and loose our tongues, helping us in an entirely new way to say: "We keep seeing the Lord!"

How good it is that you do not interpret yourself to us on the basis of how we think we see you, or how we want to see you. You are the same, yesterday, today, and forever—King of kings, born in a manger, crucified, dead, buried, eternally alive—infinitely pictured to us in the flesh and in the spirit by the very Word, of which you are the eternally Incarnate Picture.

Lord Christ, keep our eyes fixed on you, through our rapt attention to your Word and through the Spirit, who brings life and sight to it—this one Spirit, who is able to tame our fancies, discipline our curiosity, and keep us alert to the one race set before us, of which you are at once Way, Truth, and Life.

Amen

79

To everything there is a season, a time for every purpose under heaven.

—Ecclesiastes 3:1

Your Word, all sixty-six books, is jam-packed with tantalizing time warps. When we open up to Genesis, we master centuries as if there were none, and then push on to and through Exodus. How easy to pass the slow times of reality with quick-time reading. Abraham's un-mapped sojourn; conniving brothers, usurpations and deceit; soon four hundred years—almost two American histories—of cruel exile, then an exodus. How easy to jump from one miracle to another, one intervention after another, one bloody battle after another, without giving thought to the everyday, washday, workday, ordinary day, diaper washing, lentil soup distance between them. How many days of manna-eating are we willing to experience, morning by morning, gather it up, eat it, same to-morrow? Or forty years of wilderness—a whole career's worth of tented sojourn; pack up, unpack, leave next Monday; be ready to pack up again and again and again; move, stay, move; no speed-reading here, except for us—the quickly redeemed history-jumpers and promise-collectors.

Let's go ahead to Kings and Chronicles—before you know it, doz-ens of kings stand in line awaiting their three or four verses in the sun; Israel bouncing back and forth, between Jahweh and Ashtoreth, between repentance and return; seventy years of sin-earned, crushing exile, sum-marized almost like a book report. All the while, the prophets, warn-ing, preaching, pleading, straining to see ahead; false prophets speaking backwards. After that, Bible-silence, another couple American histories'-worth, sterilized with time-dumb scholar-words: The Intertestamental Period. No problem for us, though: the Savior is just around the corner. Malachi's finished and a title page later—There He Is—manger-born and ready for work.

Ready? Jesus, our very Savior, the world's salvation in manly skin, ready? History's Master and eternity's Glory, ready: his first thirty years shrink-wrapped to a few words—hardly a mention of the ten-thousand-nine-hundred-fifty-days-times-twenty-four-hours uphill climb before water went to wine (while we come unglued over a three-hour layover at LAX). But Mary, day by day, pondering and mothering; Joseph, day by day, hammering and wondering (and then probably forgetting); his Boy hammering right beside him, good with tools. His boy, Jesus himself: What were thirty years like to him, whose first urge and relentless joy was to die for us? Why the wait? What kind of give and take between patience and compulsion, between love of home and passion for the world?

Now that "It is finished," what then? A quick New Testament, just for us—ink-fresh reporting—who wouldn't want to get right at it? No; we wait some more. Years, in fact; risky years, stacking up on each other before anyone takes up pen to write those first words: "The beginning of the gospel of Jesus Christ . . . ." Words that sometimes come a bit casually: ". . . and Jesus went up to the mountain to pray . . . ." Words crafted from remembered words, no cell phone pictures, no techno-clad archivists "embedded" with the disciples, the Pharisees, the children, the lepers, the crowds, the soldiers; no, just a motley crew of wonderfully created, fully fallen and forgiven folks, taken up with zeal and living out their daily details; finally ready to write something down that we might believe, the inspiring Spirit knowing exactly when and what.

Lord, that's the way it looks sometimes, even to the most Christ-centered saints. We're spoiled. Your Word is ever so handy; it comes to us so quickly, so well ordered. Whatever pickle we're in, whatever joy overtakes us, we can "look it up" and there it is—concordance-ready—just the right verse, back in Daniel or a few hundred pages east in Acts. Here's our Bible, your Word, the ages collapsed into a spiritual catalogue to meet every situation, promise-boxes on the kitchen table, a Gideon's-worth of promises at the Days Inn.

And Lord, even when we use your Word this way, you intervene, you bless, you direct, you guide, and you smile. But Lord, what would our biblical faith be like if we began to live your Word between the written times; if we could understand, walk through, plod through, live with the slow-march between, just as we live our way through our own days; wondering when, how long, why this and not that, when will the day arrive, does it take that long, really, to get ready to do God's work, and would forty years of manna taste like forty years of fried eggs? Could we